SCOTLAND

◈ TO ◈

SHALIMAR

This is a charming book, which captures a side of our history seldom remembered; stoicism and invention in India before the dawn of the Raj, delight in the flowers and landscape, filling time during long days in a foreign land newly under British rule and a sense of cheerful duty when confronted with unexpected situations. In a way, it is my history too, illuminating the lives of many generations of my own family for whom India was home. Completely enchanting.

Joanna Lumley
OBE FRGS

All the ingredients of life, love, and cooking for generations of one British family in India before and during the Raj – I enjoyed every page.

Mary S Lovell
The Mitford Girls, The Churchills, The Riviera Set

SCOTLAND ❖ TO ❖ SHALIMAR

A Family's Life in India

Bryony Hill

Red Door

In remembrance of Ma and Roger,
children of the Raj,
with my love

Published by RedDoor
www.reddoorpress.co.uk
© 2020 Bryony Hill

978-1-913062-13-2

A CIP catalogue record for this book is available from the British Library

Cover design: Emily Courdelle
Typesetting: Megan Sheer

Printed and bound in BZGraf S.A.

CONTENTS

Part Four

Part Five

Part Six

Appendices

'Roti, mukkan, cheeni, cha
Queen Victoria bahut acha.'

'Bread, butter, sugar, tea
Queen Victoria very nice be.'

ACKNOWLEDGEMENTS

Scotland to Shalimar – A Family's Life in India emerged from an idea that has been preoccupying me for years and I wish to thank the friends and relations who helped me to get it off the ground, namely the late Brigadier Dennys Begbie, Rosemary Rawlins, and my cousin Sir Roderick Campbell (9th Baronet of Barcaldine and Glenure) in particular, who allowed me access to fascinating archive material. Anthony Stewart Smirnoff Begbie's ancestor, George Begbie, was a sibling of my two 4 x great-grandfathers, brothers Alfred and Peter Begbie, and his blog, The Begbie Archive –Tree Climbing, provided me with important military background. Last but not least, my unfathomable gratitude goes to my late uncle Roger, Ma's younger brother, who gave me the opportunity to study the precious albums at close quarters. Without his invaluable input, I would never have begun – let alone accomplished – this dream.

FOREWORD

The lives of the Britons who went out to India to found and administer the Raj, fight its battles, build its monuments and, of course, stitch it all together with an elaborate railway network, have always fascinated later generations. We remain intrigued by the miracle of so few people ruling such a vast, diverse continent, so distant from our own.

The British prior to and during the period of the Raj spent their lives in a far-off land, rarely, if ever, going home to the Old Country. Brought up to be Christians they found themselves surrounded by many different faiths, spectacular religious festivals, amazing ascetics, and evidence everywhere that there are many ways to God. Accustomed to living under the rule of one monarch they found India a patchwork of glamorous maharajas and nawabs, ruling states big and small. The countryside of the British Isles was tame and domesticated when contrasted with the massive scale of the mountains they crossed, the wide-open plains, the great rivers and the dry deserts. Then there was the ferocious heat of the Indian summer. Everyday domestic lives were complicated by a multitude of servants each ascribed one narrow task. And there was the alien food of India. Those who rejected its flavours discovered their choices were limited because so many ingredients, which constituted the familiar fare on British menus, were not available.

In *Scotland to Shalimar – a Family's Life in India* we have a record of one British family who left the Highlands for India during the reign of George

III, continuing through to the reign of Queen Victoria, the high noon of the Raj. Favourite recipes are included and are naturally fascinating, showing how those preparing meals coped with the limitations India imposed on their choice, mingled with stories of courage, sketches, photographs, riddles and rhymes, all collected through generations. It's a unique portrait of life at different stages in the ever-fascinating history of the British and their on-going relationship with India.

Sir Mark Tully KBE, former Bureau Chief of BBC, New Delhi

Nineteenth century, North Punjabi watercolour, 'Hunting wild boar'.

DRAMATIS PERSONAE

Peas Preserved Underground

Simply shell good sound peas, pack them as tightly into jars
as they go without bruising them. Seal well and bury 4ft underground.
This excludes all air and they will keep almost indefinitely.

This list of characters will give you a headache to end all headaches, but don't worry who belongs to whom – go with the flow and enjoy their story.

John Montagu, 5th Earl of Sandwich (1744–1814).
My 6 x great-grandfather

Harriet Montagu (d. 1823).
Illegitimate daughter of 5th Earl of Sandwich. Married James Grant, son of Sir Ludovic Grant, 6th Baronet of Dalvey (d. 1816).
My 5 x great-grandparents

Peter Luke Begbie (christened Patrick) (1768–1815).
Married Frances Jones (1773–1849).
My 5 x great-grandparents

Ellison Begbie (1762–1831).

Sir Duncan Campbell, 1st Baronet of Barcaldine (1786–1842).
Married Elizabeth Dreghorn Dennistoun (1793–1862).

My 4 x great-grandparents

Alfred William Begbie (1801–73). Eldest son of Peter and Frances Begbie.
Married Margaret Anna Grant of Dalvey (c. 1790–27).
Daughter of James Grant and Harriet Montagu.

*My 4 x great-grandparents. Margaret was born in India and started the
first album in the early 1800s before she married Alfred.*

Major-General Peter James Begbie (1804–64).
Son of Peter Begbie and brother of Alfred William.
Married Charlotte Morphett (1805–91).

My 4 x great-grandparents

Frances (Fanny) Charlotte Begbie (1825–74).
Daughter of Alfred William Begbie and Margaret Anna Grant.
Married Major-General John Peter William (Willie) Campbell (1824–1901),
3rd son of Sir Duncan Campbell, 1st Baronet of Barcaldine (1786–1842).

My 3 x great-grandparents

Major-General Elphinstone Waters Begbie (1842–1919).
2nd son of Major-General Peter James Begbie.

Gertrude Emma Begbie (1842–1924). Daughter of Alfred William Begbie
and his 3rd wife Margaret Watt. Married John Master.

Hilda Violet Master (1880–1969).
Daughter of Gertrude and John Master. Married Stanley Blunt, Bishop of
Bradford. Parents of (Sir) Anthony Blunt.

Lieutenant-Colonel Francis (Frank) Richard Begbie (1847–1932).
3rd son of Major-General Peter James Begbie.
Married Emily Frances Margaret Campbell, his 2nd cousin.

My great-great-grandparents

Emily Frances Margaret Campbell (1851–1930).
Daughter of Frances Charlotte and Major-General John Peter William Campbell. Married her 2nd cousin Francis Richard Begbie.
My great-great-grandparents

Sir Alexander William Campbell (Great Uncle Alick), 4th Baronet of Barcaldine (1848–1931).
Brother of Emily Frances Margaret. Never married.

Eleanor (Nell) Geraldine Begbie (1877–1951).
Daughter of Emily Frances Margaret and Frances Richard Begbie.
Married first, Colonel Alexander Harry Colvin Birch (1861–1927).
My great-grandparents. Married second, Colonel Edward (Ned) Lorimer.

Lionel Begbie (1820–1911). Brother of Eleanor Geraldine.
Charlotte (Aunt Charley) Begbie (b. 1874). Sister of Lionel
and Eleanor. Married Brigadier Cecil Barrington Norton. Sylvia, Barbara
and Phyllis. Daughters of Aunt Charley and Cecil Norton.

Douglas Birch (1900–1917). 2nd son of Nell and Alick Birch.
My great-uncle

Gerald Lorimer Birch (1913–36). Son of Nell and Ned Lorimer.
My great-uncle

Esme Margaret Birch (1897–1990). Daughter of Nell and Alick Birch.
Married Colonel Cecil Trant Shaw (1893–1960).
My maternal grandparents

Bridget Shaw (1922–2007). Daughter of Esme and Cecil Trant Shaw.
Married Trevor Jarvis. My parents

Douglas Roger Dennistoun Shaw (Roger) (1930–2017). Ma's brother.
My uncle

Paul and Neil Jarvis.
My brothers

Zandrina Pudding

*A most delicious pudding but the ingredients
must be well and separately mixed.*

Weight of 3 eggs the same size of:
butter with the salt rubbed out
the same of finely powdered sugar
same of flour
raspberry jam

Beat the butter to a cream then add the sugar, yolks of egg
and a large tablespoon of raspberry jam. Mix with the same
quantity of cold water – then add the flour. Stir all well
together and lastly pour in gently the whites of eggs beaten
to a stiff froth. Put the mixture into a mould and boil for 3
hours. Serve with jam and arrowroot sauce.

PROLOGUE

When an individual voluntarily obtrudes himself on the notice of the public, the conclusion is inevitably drawn that he either is really in possession of information hitherto not given to the world, or that he is induced by vanity to suppose that his lucubration is worthy of perusal. A brief and candid statement of my motives will best plead my apology for having ventured from the calm of private life into the arena of criticism. Madras 1834

The Malayan Peninsula, Captain (latterly Major-General) Peter James Begbie, Commander of the Madras Infantry (my 4 x great-grandfather)

Following the death of our mother Bridget in the summer of 2007, the house in Sussex where I was born had to be sold and my two brothers and I were faced with the task of clearing mountains of clutter accumulated over a period of sixty-five years. Sorting through the emotionally charged detritus of family life Ma's spirit was ever present, the sadness compounding when her haunting perfume (Givenchy's *Ysatis* – 'full of Eastern promise') wafted through every room.

One thundery afternoon, having plucked up the courage to attack the attic where bats had been roosting for decades, I made a surprising discovery when I came across a mass of letters, aerogrammes and telegrams written during WWII, which had been stored in an old gun case since 1945. The majority were sent by my father Trevor, an officer in the RNVR

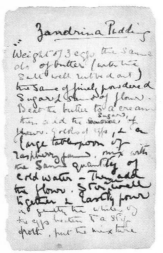

(Royal Naval Volunteer Reserve), to and from his parents, fondly nicknamed Wilbur and Jelly, when he was stationed in Ceylon (Sri Lanka), Egypt and South Africa, and taking part at Sword Beach for the Normandy landings. There was also a small bundle from Dad's younger brother Paul, a pilot officer in the RAF. Paul was shot down in his Hurricane over France only weeks before the Battle of Britain, his body and plane never found. He was twenty years old. This insightful correspondence inspired me to write *How I Long to be With You – War Letters Home* (Book Guild Publishing, November 2014).

The task nearly complete, in the dusty gloom between the cold-water tank and the eaves I spotted a cardboard box containing a crumpled package tied with string. In anticipation, the light fading fast, I undid the knot. Penned in black ink on a postcard were the words '*Zandrina pudding*'. I realised I had uncovered not long-lost love notes but a collection of my great-great-grandmother Emily Frances Margaret Campbell's recipes and those of her daughter Nell, my great-grandmother. Tinged brown with age this treasure trove preserved from their days in India where both were born in the 1800s, was scrawled on wafer-thin scraps of paper and notebooks going back more than 150 years.

In March 1987, I had travelled to New Zealand with Ma to celebrate her mother Esme's (Nell's daughter) ninetieth birthday. My grandmother produced two bulky albums. Spanning four reigns, those of George III, George IV, William IV and Queen Victoria, they were packed with pictures, poems, riddles and sketches. Dating from when the family first set foot in India at the beginning of the nineteenth century, the enchanting images and jottings came from the hands of my 3 x great-grandmother Frances Charlotte, her daughter Emily, my great-great-grandmother, Emily's husband Colonel Francis Richard Begbie, my great-great-grandfather, and Nell, my great-grandmother, alongside contributions from their friends and the military menfolk when off-duty.

Born in East Lothian in 1790, Margaret Anna Grant (my 4 x great-grandmother) started the first album circa 1818 after she arrived in India. Her mother, Harriet Montagu, was the illegitimate daughter of John Montagu, 5th Earl of Sandwich, son of the creator of the eponymous snack. Her father, James, was the son of Sir Ludovic Grant of Dalvey. James was employed by the East India Company and, in 1824, Margaret Anna married Alfred William Begbie. Once her own album was filled, their daughter Frances 'Fanny' Charlotte (my 3 x great-grandmother) carried on the tradition when she married Major-General John Peter William 'Willie' Campbell, who presented his young bride with her own blank volume on their wedding day in 1847.

Perhaps the most delightful entries are the exquisite watercolours of flowers which, hidden from harsh sunlight for two centuries, remain as fresh and vibrant as the day they were painted. Esme recounted that on the Indian subcontinent most households endeavoured to replicate productive vegetable and flower gardens in the same way they had for previous generations back home. She added that those blessed with artistic skills reproduced the fruits of their labours on paper, often with botanical accuracy. *The Calcutta Review* of 1856 endorsed this wish that, in order to relieve 'Indian ennui, we may practise painting ourselves'.

A seed was sown which germinated into this tale of young women uprooted by their heels from Britain and of those born in this foreign land with its alien culture hundreds of miles from the Old Country and so-called 'civilisation', together with their new husbands and the sports and entertainment in which they engaged to relax away from the battlefield, the civil service or the law courts. Research into my forebears was complicated by the fact that names such as Francis, Frances, Charlotte, Peter, Alfred and James cropped up everywhere, added to which, there were at least three called Augustus. The conundrum proved even more enigmatic when I divined that two of Peter and Frances Begbie's sons, Alfred and Peter, were both my 4 x great-grandfathers, each sibling linked with the Campbell family through marriage. You can only imagine the complications and pitfalls with which I was confronted and, tantamount to unravelling skeins

A wedding cake. From my cousin Sir Roderick Campbell, 9th Baronet of Barcaldine's album. John Peter William and Frances Campbell were both Roderick and my 3 x great-grandparents.

of wool entangled by a mischievous kitten, I pray that I have knitted everything together correctly without dropping too many stitches along the way. Mostly, I do not wish to bombard the reader with endless dates and names; the *Dramatis Personae* should suffice as a point of reference.

I am fully aware that there are countless books dedicated to Anglo-Indian cuisine, but the small selection of recipes (the tip of an iceberg) I have included represents the food that was cooked by my family using the ingredients available to them wherever they were stationed, be it in the Northwest Frontier, the foothills of the Himalaya, away on campaign or in the Nilgiri Hills in southern India. At first, I found it curious to see so many stews and steamed puddings on the menu, which seemed outlandish in such a testing climate, until I learned that when the family retreated to higher altitudes in order to escape the punishing summer heat on the plains, although the days were pleasant and balmy, there could be snow on the ground, the nights chilly, and hearty meals were necessary to keep body and soul together. Also, in order to retain the sense of period and authenticity, I have copied them verbatim exactly as they were jotted down by Emily and Nell. Their basic cooking tips, an explanation of Indian weights and measures, and a table of proportions can be found in the appendices.

Some recipes are more of a curiosity, others remain family favourites to this day but by their very nature they have little (if any) direction, since both mother and daughter were excellent cooks. Intelligent, indomitable women, their sense of humour and pioneering spirit leap from every page.

PART
ONE

Oatmeal Scones

6 units oatmeal or 2 of porridge oats
6 units flour
3 units sugar
1 chittack butter
2 eggs well beaten
½ breakfast cup sour milk
1 level teaspoon bicarbonate of soda
1 level teaspoon cream of tartar
1 level teaspoon Yeatman's baking powder

Mix flour, oatmeal, sugar etc. Rub in butter. Add eggs, lastly the sour milk. Make into scones and bake.

1

SCOTTISH ROOTS AND GEORGIAN BEGINNINGS

My tale begins in the mists of time in Argyll and Bute on the rugged west coast of Scotland the homeland of my ancestors the Campbells of Barcaldine and Glenure, and the Lammermuirs, the domain of the Begbies, a range of low, gentle hills forming a natural boundary between Lothian and the border with England.

My great-great-grandmother Emily Frances Margaret Begbie (neé Campbell) was fascinated by her heritage and produced a document entitled *My Grandmother* (Elizabeth Dennistoun of Dennistoun, my 4 x great-grandmother and wife of Sir Duncan Campbell, 8th of Barcaldine, 1st Baronet – 1786–1842) *Lady Campbell's Family, the Dennistouns of Dennistoun*. Motto: *Adversa virtute repello* [*Adverse power repels*].

A charter was granted by Malcolm IV of Scotland (1153–1165) in which the lands of Danzielstoun (afterwards created by Robert III into a barony) are mentioned, but the name is said to have existed before that time. In 1016 Anselan O'Cahan, son of the King of South Ulster, emigrated to Scotland and married an heiress of the name of Denniestoun. The first authentic record of Sir Hugh de Danzielstoun of that Ilk was during the reign of Alexander III (1249–1286) when he witnessed a charter granting a reluctant submission as Knight of the Shire of Renfrew to

Lady Campbell, my 4 x great-grandmother, painted by Sir Henry Raeburn.

Sir Duncan Campbell, 1st Baronet of Barcaldine and Glenure, my 4 x great-grandfather, painted by Sir Henry Raeburn.

Edward I of England (the 'Hammer of the Scots'). His name appears in the Ragman Roll [a collection of instruments by which the nobility of Scotland subscribed allegiance to Edward I] as a signatory.

His daughter Joanna (or Janet) married Sir Adam Mure of Rowallan and was the mother of Elizabeth Mure, 1st Queen of Robert III (thus an ancestress of the royal line of Stuart). The Dennistouns took an additional motto, 'Kings come of us, not we of kings'.

Finlaystone Castle (House) in Renfrewshire was the chief seat of the de Danzielstouns (Dennistouns) and was sold, she writes, to a 'Mr Graham of Glasgow for £40 000. Finlaystone House, [sic] which is surrounded by woods, stands on rising ground near the shore of the Clyde and this place was the residence of James, Earl of Glencairn, the patron of Burns [more of whom later], who wrote his famous *Lament* under an elm tree in the grounds.'

A Highland scene.

During the reigns of Robert, the Bruce and David II, Sir John de Danzielstoun married Mary, the sister of his brother-in-law the Earl of Wigton. They had many children, one of whom, Robert, 'was associated with the Earl of Glencairn in his machinations and correspondence with King Henry VIII of England and had a reversion in his favour, under the Great Seal, in 1546, of all "treasons and crimes" committed with the Earl.'

Emily goes on to explain links with our Royal family:

> John Dennistoun was prevented by his father from joining Prince Charlie's standard in 1745. He retired to England and, in 1746, took oaths to Government and became a leading American merchant. He married twice his second wife, Mary Lyon, came from a younger branch of the Glamis family – hence the Strathmore lion in the Dennistoun coat of arms.

Seven years after the Jacobite rising in 1745, Colin Roy Campbell of Glenure was involved in one of the most notorious miscarriages of justice of the time. Appointed Factor by the government to collect taxes, he was instructed to evict ardent Jacobite followers, the Stewarts of Appin (coastal area in Argyll and Bute on the west of the Scottish Highlands), from their estates. In spite of the unpalatable nature of his work Colin was generally respected and regarded as a good man. However, on 14 May 1752, whilst riding through the woods of Lettermore near Ballachulish, he was felled by a single rifle shot in the back, killing him instantly. The finger of suspicion pointed in the direction of Alan Breck Stewart, who had previously voiced threats against Colin, and who fled the area before he could be apprehended. For want of a scapegoat, James Stewart (James of the Glen, Alan Breck's foster father) was arrested in his place. As luck would have it the judge appointed to head the trial was Archibald, 3rd Duke of Argyll, Chief of Clan Campbell, and, to compound James Stewart's misery, eleven out of the fifteen members of the jury were Campbells. The poor man didn't stand a chance and, although he vociferously proclaimed his innocence with a viable alibi, he was hanged, his body left to rot on the gibbet by the Ballachulish ferry as a warning to passers-by. During the ensuing weeks, the family gathered his bones as they fell to the ground with the intention of eventually giving him a proper burial. Over a hundred years later the Appin murder inspired not only Robert Louis Stevenson in his novel *Kidnapped* but also Sir Walter Scott when he wrote *Rob Roy*.

Emily continued to tie up bloodlines through marriage to King Robert II and James II of Scotland:

Esme, so like the young Queen Mother.

Elizabeth Dreghorn Dennistoun [1793–1862, Emily's grandmother] was a daughter of James Dennistoun and Margaret Dreghorn and was related therefore collaterally and by descent with our reigning Royal family of whom her descendants today are cousins 20 times removed. She was also descended from Sir William Wallace. She married Sir Duncan Campbell of Barcaldine and Glenure, Baronet, in 1815. The present Duchess of York [the future Queen Elizabeth The Queen Mother] is descended from the youngest daughter of Robert II and Elizabeth Mure. (See Burke [Burke's Peerage] Strathmore, Earl of).

The gene pool must be strong because Esme closely resembled Queen Elizabeth The Queen Mother at a similar age.

Mrs Shallard's Marmalade

To every 3lb of cut fruit put 5lb sugar.
To every 1lb of sugar put 1 gill water.

Put the oranges whole into a saucepan and cover with cold water. Let them boil till soft changing the water after an hour and a half boiling. The oranges must be perfectly soft so that the head of a pin will pierce the fruit easily. Cut up the oranges into small pieces or slices taking out the pips. Put sugar and water into a saucepan and let it boil for 8 or 10 minutes till the syrup is clear. Then put in the fruit. Stir well and boil for 40 minutes or a little longer. Excellent.

2

ROBERT BURNS, SCOTLAND'S GREATEST POET

The name Begbie may have originated from the Old Norse for 'settlement' or 'field', so it is likely that there is more than a drop of Viking blood coursing through my own veins. Alexander Begbie (1725–83) a tenant farmer and his wife Margaret produced more than a dozen children, one of whom, Ellison (also known as Alison), was born in 1762 followed in 1768 by a brother (my 5 x great-grandfather) who, although christened Patrick Luke, was known as Peter. In 1780 when Ellison was nineteen, it is alleged she captured the heart of Robert Burns, Scotland's most celebrated poet. There has been much discussion as to the content of letters written supposedly by Burns to Ellison and no positive conclusion has come about to date. However, I am an eternal romantic and like to believe that my ancestor did find solace temporarily with the poet.

Robert, three years her senior, lived in Lochlea, a village not far from the Begbie farmstead in Haddestone and their passionate relationship inspired him to embark upon an effusive, devoted correspondence. In one of his letters to Ellison,[1] he wrote:

---

1 Copyright: Project Gutenberg EBook of the letters to Robert Burns by Robert Burns.

All these charming qualities [in Ellison] heightened by an education much beyond anything I have ever met in any woman I ever dared to approach, have made an impression on my heart that I do not think the world can ever efface. I can only say I sincerely love you, and there is nothing on earth I so ardently wish for, or that could possibly give me so much happiness, as one day to see you mine.

Surprisingly, Robert seemed to lack confidence.

Though I be, as you know very well, but a very awkward lover myself, yet, as I have some opportunities of observing the conduct of others who are much better skilled in the affair of courtship than I am, I often think it is owing to lucky chance, more than to good management, that there are not more unhappy marriages than usually are. I hope, my dear Ellison, you will do me the justice to believe me, when I assure you that the love I have for you is founded on the principles of virtue and honour, and by consequence so long as you continue possessed of those admirable qualities which first inspired my passion for you, so long I must continue to love you. Believe me my dear, it is love like this alone, which can render the marriage state happy.

There are further outpourings of adoration.

Oh! Happy state, when souls each other draw, where love is liberty, and nature law. I know, were I to speak in such a style to many a girl, who thinks herself possessed of no small share of sense, she would think it ridiculous – but the language of the heart is, my dear Ellison, the only courtship I shall ever use to you.

His poem *The Lass of Cessnock Banks* emanated from Burns's deep feelings for Ellison, which also inspired the character Peggy Alison of *Ilk care and fear, when thou art near* ('Bonnie Peggy Alison'). In *The Songs of Burns for Voice and Pianoforte* (1896) by John Kenyon Lees, the author states that in this song, 'the heroine of "this song of similes" was

Ellison Begbie, whom Burns vainly endeavoured to win for his wife. The song, Mr Chambers [Robert, editor] notes, appeared for the first time in Cromek's "Reliques", the editor stating that he had recovered it "from the oral communication of a lady residing in Glasgow, whom the bard in early life affectionately admired." Mr Chambers says it seem not unlikely that Ellison herself had grown into this lady.'

With regard to Burns's song, 'Mary Morison', that author continues, 'The various editors of the poet have puzzled their brains to fit a heroine to the song, and Mr W Scott Douglas decides that "Mary Morison" is none other than the Ellison Begbie to whom Burns addressed his earliest love letters. Burns pays tribute to "amiable goodness" in his final letter to Ellison Begbie.'

This extract from another letter confirms the above and is virtually a proposal:

> If you will be so good and so generous as to admit me for your partner, your companion, your bosom friend through life, there is nothing on this side of eternity shall give me greater transport. I can only say I sincerely love you, and there is nothing on earth I so ardently wish for, or that could possibly give me so much happiness, as one day to see you mine. I shall only add, further, that if behaviour, regulated (though perhaps but very imperfectly) by the rules of honour and virtue, if a heart devoted to love and esteem you, and an earnest endeavour to promote your happiness; if these are qualities you would wish in a friend, in a husband, I hope you shall ever find them in your real friend and sincere lover.

For whatever reason, Ellison rejected Robert and in June 1781 he wrote:

> I ought in good manners to have acknowledged the receipt of your letter before this time, but my heart was so shocked with the contents of it that I can scarcely yet collect my thoughts so as to write to you on the subject. I will not attempt to describe what I felt on receiving your letter. I read it over and over, again and again, and though it was in the politest language of refusal, yet it was peremptory.

You were 'sorry' you 'could not make a return' but you wish me 'all kind of Happiness'. It would be weak and unmanly to say that without you I never can be happy; but, sure I am that sharing life with you would have given it a relish that, wanting you, I can never taste.

My twenty-third year was to me an important era. Partly through whim, and partly that I wished to set about doing something in life, I joined a flax-dresser in a neighbouring town [Irvine] to learn his trade.

Unfortunately matters did not pan out as he hoped and Robert considered his partner a 'scoundrel of the first water; and to finish the whole, as we were giving a welcome carousal to the New Year, the shop took fire and burnt to ashes, and I was left, like a true poet, not worth a sixpence.' Still stinging from Ellison's rejection, he continued 'and, to crown my distresses, a *belle fille*, whom I adored, and who had pledged her soul to meet me in the field of matrimony, jilted me, with peculiar circumstances of mortification.'

On 12 June 1781 Burns wrote to William Niven, his friend from schooldays:

> I am entirely got rid of all connections with the tender sex, I mean in the way of courtship; it is, however absolutely certain that I am so; though how long I shall continue so, Heaven only knows. But be that as it may, I shall never be involved as I was again.

In spite of this, Robert recovered when he met and fell in love with Jean Armour, who bore him two sets of twins prior to their wedding in 1788. They went on to have six more children one of whom, a son (b. 1794), was christened James Glencairn. When he died aged seventy-two, his obituary in *The Elevator, Volume 1, Number 43,* dated 26 January 1866, explains his unusual second name:

> He was named James Glencairn after James [Cunningham], late [14th] Earl of Glencairn, Robert Burns' lifelong friend [and patron]. It was through Lord Glencairn that James obtained a commission in the Madras Army in which he rose to a distinguished rank.

Ellison's nephew, Peter James Begbie (Peter Luke's son, my 4 x great-grandfather), was a major-general and in command of the Madras Infantry and it is possible that the friendship between Ellison and Robert continued and helped in securing the posting. James had a good career in the army, mentioned in the *East India Military Calendar,* under the article dated 17 March 1820:

> Camp Lumba [situated in the Province of Gujarat] Brigadier Knox takes the earliest opportunity to offer his cordial thanks to the whole of the troops he had the honour to command before Lamba... and his best thanks are also due to Capt C Taylor, Major of the Brigade, and Lieut J G Burns, Commissariat Office. After a career of honours in India Col J G Burns [as James Glencairn subsequently became] returned to England to live with his brother in Cheltenham.

The watercolour of the Taj Mahal with its accompanying verse signed J G Burns was a contribution by Robert's son James with his wife Jean Armour, to Margaret Anna's album and shows the link between the Begbies and Robert continued.

Watercolour of the Taj Mahal and poem by James Glencairn Burns.

Uncle Tom

Mix 15 units of flour into ¼ unit bicarbonate of soda and 10 units of chopped suet. Make into a stiff paste with 2 ½ units milk and 2 ½ units golden syrup. Steam in a tightly covered mould for 2 hours. Leave plenty of room for it to rise. Serve with custard and more golden syrup. By adding a little sugar, raisins, peel an admirable children's pudding can be made.

3

HEADING
SOUTH OF THE BORDER

In 1797, Ellison's brother Peter Luke married Frances Jones, the tenth child of thirteen. Frances was born south of the border in Reigate Priory, Surrey. In 1541, following the Dissolution of the Monasteries, Henry VIII gave this estate to Lord William Howard, the uncle of Henry's fifth wife Catherine, after which it was converted to a family dwelling.

Two centuries later and three years after her husband died in 1780, Frances's mother Ann inherited the priory from an uncle Richard Ireland. A prosperous cheese merchant, Richard purchased the handsome thirteenth-century manor house and its (then) 76 acres of parkland at auction in 1766 for £4000 (approximately £700 000 in today's money). According to Eileen Wood, Curator of Reigate Priory Museum, 'a detailed survey of the estate was carried out during Richard's ownership and the original document is one of our prized possessions. Following a fire in one of the wings, Richard Ireland made many alterations to the building and changed its appearance.'

In the *Autobiography of William Jerdan* (Editor of *The Literary Gazette*) the author writes:

> For several years, previous to this period of my life, I lived on very intimate terms with a much-respected gentleman Mr Peter Begbie,

Above left: *Frances Begbie (neé Jones), my 5 x great-grandmother.* Above right: *Peter (Patrick Luke) Begbie, my 5x great-grandfather.*

who had been in the Indian mercantile service and now held a peculiar official situation in Somerset House [working in the Stamp Office, a government department dealing with taxes]. A numerous family surrounded his hospitable domestic hearth [Peter and Frances's first son Alfred William made his appearance in 1801, followed by another sibling in 1804 named Peter James, then further offspring over the ensuing years]– the daughters accomplished with fine natural attainments – and his sons acquiring that instruction which was to forward them in their several walks of life, chiefly the church and the military and civil service of India. All the three elder girls (Anne, Margaret Helen and Fanny) wrote sweet poetry for *The Sun* [a semi-Tory paper of which Jerdan was also the editor] and many of their compositions afterwards adorned *The Literary Gazette*, as I shall have occasion to notice in due time.

William Jerdan had great respect for the writing talents of Peter and Frances's daughters:

Reigate Priory.

Peter.

Frances.

Preliminary sketches by George Henry Harlow of my 4 x great-grandfather Alfred William Begbie, for the painting 'Hubert and Prince Arthur'.

In the narrative portion of my work I have mentioned the contributions of other fair and gifted poetesses, many of them worthy of a less ephemeral sphere, and more distinct appropriation to their writers. But I fear the hope of such a just decree is in vain. Among the number, connected by friendship and family ties, were three daughters of my friend Mr Begbie, Anne, Margaret Helen and Fanny, all of whom displayed fine tastes and feelings; and the same may be recorded of Dr Croly [the Rev. Dr George Croly], whose poetry helped greatly to establish the repute of the paper in its earlier years, when poetry was not a drug but a pleasure!

[George Henry] Harlow, whom I introduced to them, painted portraits of them, and fancy pieces in which they figured, for his *Hubert and Prince Arthur* and *King John* [exhibited in 1815], my friend Begbie and his eldest son [Alfred] sat for the characters.

Jerdan expounds about his social connections with Peter, with whom he met...

at least twice a week and many a happy day I spent in their company [Peter's wife Frances and their children] but – there is always a but – a serious misfortune sprung out of this enjoyment and afforded exactly such an incident as is likely to affect the welfare of a literary man. Among the acceptable and intelligent gentlemen with whom I became acquainted at Mr Begbie's was Mr Whitehead, the principal of the banking firm Whitehead, Howard and Haddock, of money I then possessed. On 17th of November, this old established and highly respectable house, connected with many country banks, was compelled to stop payment; and notwithstanding the first favourable report of assets, and the known

Hubert and Prince Arthur, painted by George Henry Harlow, for whom Peter and Alfred posed.

43

Left: *Pencil sketch of Napoleon Bonaparte from Margaret Anna's album.*

Below: *Poem by William Collins (1721–59) in 1746 to honour those American and British soldiers who made the ultimate sacrifice for their nation and which became one of the best known poems in the eighteenth century.*

How sleep the brave who sink to rest
By all their country's wishes blest,
When spring with dewy fingers cold,
Returns to their hallowed mould,
She there shall dress a sweeter sod,
Than Fancy's feet have ever trod.
By Fairy hands their knell is rung,
By forms unseen their dirge is sung.
There Honour comes, a pilgrim grey,
To bless the turf that wraps their clay;
And Freedom shall a while repair,
To dwell, a weeping hermit, there!

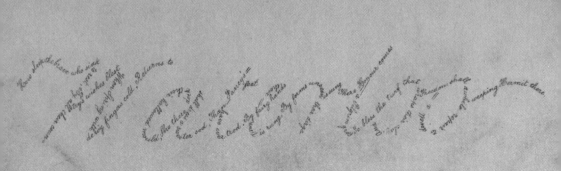

worth and integrity of the partners, the hope entertained of a favourable winding up was never fulfilled.

Another casualty following the demise of Whitehead, Howard and Haddock, Peter was declared bankrupt. Susan Matoff, in her book *The Account of a Conflicted Life: W Jerdan (1782–1869), London Editor, Author and Critic* (Sussex Academic Press, 2010), says: 'Jerdan lodged his hard-won savings with the bank.' It took him years to recover from this financial loss but his 'beloved friend' Peter never overcame such a personal disaster.

Jerdan wrote:

> I learnt that Mr Begbie, like a good Samaritan as he was, had humanely taken charge of him (Mr Whitehead) in his distraction and accompanied him to Calais.

Peter contacted Jerdan from France:

> Poor Whitehead! How I feel for him for, though prepared for the event, yet he was not without hopes that the house might have weathered the storm. I fear he has not the nerves to return. I wish to God, my friend, you and Mrs B [Frances] could induce Mrs W to join us as soon as she can. Till she does, I cannot leave him. I do firmly believe that I have saved his life. As far as I can be comfortable away from my family I am so, but it is painful the state of suspense.
>
> On the 10th March [1815] a thunderclap burst upon an astonished Europe:
>
> Buonaparte [sic] had escaped from Elba, and landed in France!

Peter died in 1815, the same year as the Battle of Waterloo. Jerdan reports his passing in *The Literary Gazette*:

> Before the end of the year, as previously mentioned, I had the unhappiness to lose my much-esteemed friend Mr Begbie. He had been removed for change to a pleasant villa at North End, Hammersmith but,

all in vain. Early in December he died, leaving a widow and numerous offspring very unsatisfactorily provided for and Peter was declared bankrupt. But she [Frances] was a woman of a strong and energetic mind, and fortunately for her children, could do for them, through near relatives (especially her mother, Mrs Jones) and other friends, what her husband withheld by his position and independent feelings from soliciting. His considerable income expired with him; but not the friendships of those whom his excellent nature and honourable conduct had attached to him and who now displayed that attachment by bestowing valuable appointments on his sons, and launching them with favourable prospects on the world.

Frances, in her letter to Mr Jerdan, wrote:

My poor husband has been in the agonies of death all night, and we expected his dissolution every minute. I will not tell you what I have suffered. Whenever he thought himself dying he called me to him, to bid him farewell, and to let him 'die in my arms'. This morning he has recovered a little, and lies tolerably composed, and Mr West (the medical adviser) thinks he may linger yet another night. If you are well enough to come to me on your return, do. He thinks he could die in peace if he heard you were likely to succeed in your generous intentions. To prevent unnecessary fatigue to you, and alarm to Mrs Jerdan, do not think of returning at night; I can give you a bed, and indeed I have much to say to you, and consult you about. Mr West has promised to spend the night here he was in the house from four o'clock till nine.

By giving laudanum, my dear Peter does not seem in those violent agonies; he is quite calm, and prays to be released from his sufferings. My poor girls and Alfred (the eldest son) are also quite broken-hearted.[2] [***] has fainted away [***] it is truly a house [***] of mourning – how I hold up I cannot imagine; but for my beloved

2   *** The letter is here defaced by the seal.

'Humdrum' painted by James Prinsep, 1823.

children I think I should sink under my troubles. I do not know that I could go through such another night – to see my poor husband in danger of suffocation – to hear his groans – to hear him pray, for me and my children – indeed it was too much; but I will not agonise your feeling heart, which I know participates largely in my sorrows.

Adieu. Yours truly,
Frances Begbie

Frances continues her correspondence from their family home in Northend, on 5 December:

My dear Sir, your truly kind and generous conduct to me and mine, entitles you to my warmest gratitude. It is impossible for me to thank you but the approbation of your own heart will, I trust, be an ample reward.

Never did consolation arrive at a time when it was more wanted. Just as I got your letter, my poor suffering husband appeared to be nearly expiring. Even while I write you will hardly know from his countenance that he existed; he has the hiccups incessantly and, perhaps, ere you receive[3] [***] you get this [***] he may be no more. Never can I sufficiently thank Mr Freeling for his kindness. Tell him he has, by his generous endeavours to serve me, and my helpless children, rescued me almost from despair. Without the help of some friends, I could not support the mournful situation I am at present in. May the Almighty Being who has warmed your liberal heart to assist me and mine, return the generous act tenfold upon you and your family.

Frances writes to Jerdan with sad news:

Wednesday morning.

All your poor friend's troubles are over; He ceased to breathe at twenty minutes past ten this night, without a struggle or a groan. [Mr Jerdan writes, 'The final details need not be repeated'.]

William Jerdan continues in *The Literary Gazette*:

Writerships [sic], cadetcies [sic] and other auspicious provisions were made, and the family resources of Mrs Begbie sufficed for the rest. At first however, there was much to suffer; and I am not without hope that it will tend to redeem my course from some of its faults if I venture to show that, in this, as in many another instance, my character from youth to age, was genial, kindly of heart and rejoicing in privilege of doing good when in my power. Such also was my lamented friend whose liberality of mind and generosity of sentiment had made him a much poorer man than he ought to have been. I do not believe he ever committed a wrong or did wilful injury to man, woman or child, but his worth, combined with an easiness of temperament, was not an adequate

3 *** The letter is defaced by the seal.

protection for his open purse and honest heart. He contributed much valuable information, chiefly commercial, to *The Sun*.

Francis Feeling (later Baronet of Ford and Hutchings in the County of Sussex for services to the General Post Office) wrote to Jerdan 'Your letters do great credit to your feelings – poor Begbie!'

Above left: *Peter.*

Above right: *Frances.*

Meat Curry

For curry to be good, it must take 2 hours at least to make.

1 unit curry powder
4 units peeled and sliced onions
1 teaspoonful salt
½lb beef, mutton, lamb or pork

Cut beef into one inch squares. All other meat may be cut in the same way in neat pieces. Heat ghee in a saucepan and fry half the onions till brown. Add curry powder and fry together for 3 or 4 minutes. Add salt and ¼ pint hot water, stir well then add another ¼ pint hot water and let the whole boil fast without stirring for a few minutes, or until it begins to stick on the bottom of the pan. Do not let it burn. Add ½ pint more hot water, stir and add meat and the rest of the onions. Stir well and simmer till meat is tender and fully cooked. The addition of ¼ pint of cold milk may be added at the same time as the meat is an improvement – the water proportionately reduced. For beef curry add sprigs of fennel. Curries may be varied by the addition of vegetables.

Madras Curry Paste

8 units of:
coriander (*dhaniya*)
turmeric (*haldee*)
cumin (*jeera*)
4 units of:
pepper (*mirch*)
dry sugar (*sookhee cheeri*)
2 units of:
fenugreek (*menthee*)
cardamoms (*sarason ke bee*)
clover (*kaung*)

Mix all the ingredients well together. Excellent!

4

CROSSING CONTINENTS AND NEW FRIENDSHIPS

Peter James Begbie, until he was sixteen years old, was educated at Edinburgh High School after which he opted to pursue a military career when he was accepted by the East India Army Training Academy at Addiscombe in Surrey. Formed in 1809 (and closed in 1861) it was the training ground for young officers to serve in the East India Company's (EIC) private army in India. The city of Madras (Chennai) was created in 1640 to serve the trading interests of the EIC. In January 1823 Peter James followed in his older brother Alfred William's footsteps by travelling to India, landing in Calcutta (Kolkata) where Alfred was there to meet him.

Peter joined the Madras Artillery at Fort George. On 10 May 1823, at the age of nineteen, he was commissioned as Second Lieutenant and, the following day, promoted to full Lieutenant. In 1833, he was promoted to Captain, Major in 1846, finally ending up as brevet (temporary) Major-General in command of the entire establishment. His career led him to be employed with the Jaulnah Light Field Force in the southern Mahratta country during the Siege of Kittor (1824–25) and he was a participant in the East India Company's wars against Burma in 1824–26, for which he was awarded both the Burma Medal and the India Medal for Ava (the dominant kingdom in Upper Burma). On 3 July 1826 in Madras, Peter James married Charlotte Ward Morphett, a girl

Major-General Peter James Begbie my 4 x great-grandfather.

from Mallow, County Cork. They had four children: Charlotte Elizabeth, Elphinstone Waters, Francis Richard and Alfred Daniel.

On 24 October 1818 in Trichinopoly (a district of the erstwhile presidency of Madras), Peter's sister Anne married Edward James Foote, a captain in the 18th Madras Native Infantry. A year later another sister Margaret Helen married the aforementioned (by William Jerdan, who wrote of his talent for poetry) Rev. Dr George Croly, a preacher at the church of St Stephen's in Walbrook in the City of London, whose oratory skills were praised in *The Lady's Garland and Family Magazine*. 'Dr Croly's style of preaching is characterised by impressive eloquence'.

This formidable reputation reached as far north as Haworth in Yorkshire and succeeded in enticing sisters Charlotte and Anne Bronte, when in London in 1846, to visit the church in the hope of enjoying his address, only to be disappointed to learn that Dr Croly was not conducting the service that day.

This is an extract taken from the *The Gentleman's Magazine*, following the Reverend's demise in November 1860:

In 1819, Mr Croly, in Kensington Church, married Margaret Helen Begbie, the daughter of a much-respected Scottish gentleman [Peter Luke] who had been in the East India trade, but died the holder of an office under the Board of Trade, which had some supervision of ship assurances. A family of six children, five sons and a daughter, were the fruit of the union. The eldest son was unfortunately killed in 1845 in one of the battles with the Sikhs.

One of the last watercolours in Margaret Anna's album is of the *Petrifying Falls at Dehra Dhun* (sic) signed, G A Croly, XXVIth LI (18th Light Infantry), 29th September 1845. I discovered the artist was Lieutenant George Alfred Croly of the 26th Bengal Native Infantry, the Reverend Croly and Margaret Helen's eldest son. Another painting by George hangs in the National Army Museum in London entitled, *The Road to Kabul, (First Afghan War 1839–42) Fort of Al-Musjid, Khyber Pass Camp of the 4th Brigade of Maj-Gen Pollock's Force, April 1842*. Poignantly, less than three months after contributing to Margaret Anna's album, George was involved in the 1st Sikh War (1845–46) and was killed in action at the Battle of Ferozeshah, a small village in the Punjab. It was arguably the most brutal confrontation the British had experienced in India: around 5000 Sikhs were either killed or wounded and, although the British had heavy losses of 1,800 men, they were victorious. Lieutenant Croly was twenty-three years old.

A particularly prolific contributor to the first album was James Prinsep (1799–1840), whom Margaret Anna met through his younger brother Augustus, the young men being contemporaries at Haileybury School in Hertfordshire, as was her future husband Alfred. The East India College, Haileybury was founded in 1806 as a pool to provide the Honourable East India Company with candidates to govern British India along with junior servants known as 'writers'. These young men were trained to record all accounting, minutes of meetings, data recovered from ships' logs, and to correspond by letter with London, all

Watercolour of the Petrifying Falls at Dehra Dhun, painted by Lieutenant George Alfred Croly, XXVIth LI, 1845.

written in triplicate to ensure safe arrival: two were sent by separate ships and the third overland. Circa 1800 a handbill was issued to each selected 'writer' listing items to be purchased prior to departure for India:

> A book of Arabian poetry, a Persian dictionary, tobacco, wax candles, and all sorts of clothes including striped gingham trousers, cashmere breeches, fancy waistcoats and fine hats.

This would have been a considerable cost to each individual whose annual salary at the time amounted to £5. *The Calcutta Review*, 1856 says:

> Finance is a subject which has been omitted almost entirely in the preparatory training which they [the students] undergo. During his residence at Haileybury the student is not indoctrinated with the great principles of that political science. The moral sciences, the classics, the mathematics, history and languages have all received their share of attention but finance is not even hinted at by those gentlemen.

The Monthly Magazine Vol. 49 reports:

> On 3rd December, a deputation of the Court of Directors of the East India Company proceeded to the college at Haileybury for the purpose of receiving the report of the results of the general examination of the students, at the close of term. The students, as usual, read and translated from Sanskrit, Arabic, Persian and Hindustani languages. Prizes were then delivered.

When a student at Haileybury Alfred received accolades, reported in *The London Gazette* on 28 May 1819, 'the prize for Bengallee [sic] and with great credit in other departments.' Augustus Prinsep, [brother of James] was awarded 'a prize of books in Hindustani and in English composition.'

In September 1812, when both were twenty years old, Alfred and James (Prinsep) landed in Calcutta. Alfred was employed by the British Civil Service until 1819 before joining the Indian Civil Service. This change of career was extremely beneficial having been engaged as Assistant Magistrate of the North Division of Bundelkhand in February 1821, followed by the appointment of Civil and Session Judge in the North-Western Provinces and finally being elevated to Lieutenant-Governor of the same in 1853.

His marriage to Margaret Anna was announced in *The London Gazette* dated 30 August 1824:

> At Allahabad, A W Begbie Esq, Civil Service, to Margaret Anna, daughter of the late James Grant Esq, formerly of this Service.

Tragically, Margaret Anna died three years later in 1827, in Humeerpore (Hamirpur, in the Himalayan state of Himachal Pradesh), leaving her husband to care for their two-year-old daughter Frances (Fanny) Charlotte, my 3 x great-grandmother. According to certain records Alfred married again in June 1831, this time to Charlotte Augusta Rickets who also passed away not long afterwards, in 1833. Then, in 1836 in Allahabad, he married Margaret Watt and they had a daughter, Gertrude Emma. Margaret was his third wife to die but, not one to remain single, Alfred ventured for a fourth time down the aisle when he married Lucy Sharp in Shimla in October 1848.

Rock Cakes

4 units butter
4 units sugar
16 units flour
8 units currants and sultanas, mixed
2 units candied peel
lemon peel
4 units eggs
a little milk
Mix together. The paste must be very stiff. Using a
dessertspoon, place rough, rocky lumps onto a greased
baking sheet and dust with caster sugar.

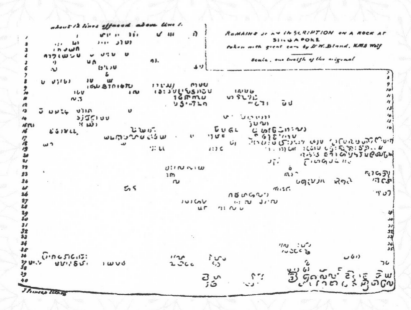

Lithograph of the Singapore Stone by James Prinsep.

5

THE SINGAPORE STONE

Away from army matters Peter James Begbie could not resist the opportunity to undertake a unique project: that of deciphering enigmatic lettering engraved on an ancient piece of sandstone discovered in June 1819 in the jungle during tree clearing. In his book *The Malayan Peninsula* (1834), Peter made 'an attempt to throw some light upon a subject so confessedly obscure'.

This fragment of a much larger slab had stood at the mouth of the Singapore River, but before Peter became involved Sir Stamford Raffles, having recently arrived on the island, was one of the first to try to identify the hitherto unrecognised alphabet, dating possibly to the thirteenth century or earlier, even as far back as the tenth century. In an attempt to make the characters more legible Sir Stamford applied a strong acid solution, which not only proved unsuccessful but complicated matters by further damaging the fragile stone.

In 1843 the original stone slab was blown up to widen the mouth of the Singapore River in order to accommodate a fort and quarters for the commander. Family friend James Prinsep was an Anglo-Indian scholar and antiquary who had studied under Augustus Pugin, the architect responsible for the interior design of the Palace of Westminster in London. James contracted an infection which damaged his eyesight and, in 1832, in the service of the East India Company, he was appointed Assay Master of the India Government Mint in Benares, a position found through his

Allahabad
18th October 1821 –

Abrupt upon the perpendic'lar bank
Of holy Jumna, stands the Bold Veranda;
Reckless of danger from the rising flood
Or from the crumbling precipices: Sweet spot
For meditating maids to parley with the Moon!
Now as she vaults above yon ancient walls
As though escaping from imprisonment
Within their gloomy bastions:– while thro' fear
Her quiv'ring moonbeam magnifies twofold
The stony mass of dungeon she surmounts!–
      The Evening Gun – hark how its harsh rebound
Wakes to a moment's life the slumb'ring scene;
Warning yon girl romantic with the Harp
That bedtime is approach'd:– or that the tea
Is getting cold" – unpicturesque idea!–
Yet lingers there one youth upon that Terrace
In melancholy posture, with his eye
Turned to the twinkling lights at Qilla Ghât:
There his imagination sees distinct
A damsel fairer than the cloudless moon,
Tending with filial care her aged father!
How can he close his eyes, when his adored
Passes a watchful night? tomorrow morn
That Pinnace shall have vanish'd:– let him take
One last long lingering look, then – go to bed!

'Allahabad' painted by James Prinsep, 1821.

father. Devoted to Indian inscriptions and numismatics, he reformed the complex system of Indian weights and measures and introduced a uniform coinage. James was another ideal candidate to try to unravel the stone and when he received the devastating news of its destruction (some of it ground down to gravel to use in the construction of a road) he asked the Governor of the Straits Settlements, Colonel William Butterworth, to secure any remaining legible fragments, ensuring that they were transported to be preserved in the Asiatic Society's museum in Calcutta. In his letter, Butterworth wrote:

> The only remaining portion of the stone, I have found lying in the veranda of the Treasury at Singapore, where it was used as a seat by the sepoys [formerly the term given to an Indian soldier in the service of a European power] of the guard and persons waiting to transact business.

There has been much deliberation as to the origin of the inscription. John Crawfurd (1783–1868) described the slab in his journal on 3 February 1822 in these terms[4]:

> On the stony point which forms the western side of the entrance of the salt creek, on which the modern town of Singapore is building, there was discovered, two years ago, a tolerably hard block of sand-stone, with an inscription upon it. This I examined early this morning. The stone, in shape, is a rude mass, and formed of the one-half of a great nodule broken into two nearly equal parts by artificial means; for the two portions now face each other, separated at the base by a distance of not more than two feet and a half, and reclining opposite to each other at an angle of about forty degrees. It is upon the inner surface of the stone that the inscription is engraved. The workmanship is far ruder than anything of the kind that I have seen in Java or India; and the writing, perhaps from time, in some degree, but more from the natural

---

4 *Journal of an Embassy from the Governor General of India to the Courts of Siam and Cochin, India; Exhibiting a View of the Actual State of Those Kingdoms. Kuala Lumpur*, by Crawfurd, J, 1828.

'Making progress in chemistry', by James Prinsep.

'About to start for Benares' by James Prinsep, 1821.

decomposition of the rock, so much obliterated as to be quite illegible as a composition. Here and there, however, a few letters seem distinct enough. The character is rather round than square.

James started the *Journal of the Asiatic Society of Bengal* in which, in 1837, he published a paper by a Dr William Bland of HMS *Wolf* stating that he had made a facsimile of all that remained in any way perceptible on the slab. Dr Bland described the slab thus:

> On a tongue of land forming the termination of the right bank of the river at Singapore, now called Artillery Point, stands a stone or rock of coarse red sandstone about ten feet high, from two to five feet thick, and about nine or ten feet in length, somewhat wedge-shaped, with weather-worn cells. The face sloping to the south-east at an angle of 76° has been smoothed down in the form of an irregular square, presenting a space of about thirty-two square feet, having a raised edge all round.
>
> On this surface, an inscription has originally been cut, of about fifty lines, but the characters are so obliterated by the weather that the greater part of them are illegible. Still, there are many left which are plain enough, more particularly those at the lower right-hand corner, where the raised edge of the stone has in some measure protected them.

To date, no one has been able to come to a successful conclusion as to its origin.

In time, James's clear vision returned enabling him to design, amongst other edifices, a church and the new mint building at Benares. Other health problems emerged and, in November 1838, he set sail for England where, two years later, he died in London whilst staying at his sister's house in Westminster.

Half-Pay Pudding

An egg may be used, but then only half the quantity of milk. To make it more economical, add 1 cup of cold tea – this gives very good results.

1 cup flour
1 teaspoonful salt
1 teaspoonful bicarbonate of soda
1 cup fresh white breadcrumbs
1 cup dark (muscovada) sugar
1 cup of suet
1 cup mixed dried fruit: sultanas, raisins, currants
zest of ½ a lemon

Mix all the dry ingredients together. Blend the milk with the bicarbonate of soda and add to the other ingredients, mixing well. Pour into a buttered pudding basin and steam for 2½ – 3 hours. Serve with a sweet sauce.

6

CRAG PICKET

A nd yet England's cavalry is filled with idle men of fashion, younger sons of peers, or elder sons of stockbrokers, all ready enough for a Balaclava charge, all averse to Balaclava stable duty. In India, if possible, the case is worse. England's Cavalry is officered by volunteers, by men who select their line but India's stable horsemen are led by the boys who fail at Haileybury, and the lads whose parents have most interest in the India House. Whether they are half blind, whether they can or cannot ride, or whether they like or dislike their profession, there they remain, Cavalry officers for the duration of their service.

The Calcutta Review, 1856

On 14 October 1847, Alfred and Margaret Anna's daughter Fanny married John Peter William Campbell, the son of Sir Duncan Campbell, 1st Baronet of Barcaldine and Glenure and Elizabeth Dreghorn Dennistoun.

Willie was a Gurkha for part of his military career; for the rest, he served in the Bengal Staff Corps where he rose to the rank of Major-General.

His distinguished service record is detailed in the family book of *Records of Clan Campbell in the Service of the Honourable East India Company, 1600–1858*, which includes this anecdote:

Above: *John Peter William Campbell (on right), 1862, my 3 x great-grandfather.*

Right: *Frances Charlotte Campbell, my 3 x great-grandmother.*

Above: *Major-General John Peter William Campbell.*

Left: *Frances Campbell with her children Charlotte, Bessie and Great-Uncle Alick, 4th Baronet of Barcaldine.*

ILLUSTRATIONS OF THE VERB

"To Struggle":— "To throw one's Arms & Legs about violently."

1. Shews some Natives throwing their arms & legs about, but whether they are "struggling" to get at the Moon, or not, is left to the Imagination.

2. Depicts a gentleman also throwing his arms & legs about, but what he is struggling for, the sketch sheweth not. [Happy Thought! Perhaps he is "struggling" to keep his temper!]

3. Portrays a Scotchman, who is evidently "struggling" to be happy under the adverse circumstances of doing the "Highland Fling" over some thistles.

4. Sketch of "Ye Streete Arabe" "struggling" for his living.

━━━━━━━ ━━━━━━━

5. Illustration intended to convey the meaning — "to contend".

6. Sheweth a man "struggling" along under the weight of a heavy portmanteau.

7. Illustrates the verb "to struggle" as meaning "to strive"

8. "He struggled to forget," by the baneful use of Opium

By Francis Richard Begbie, my 3 x great-grandfather

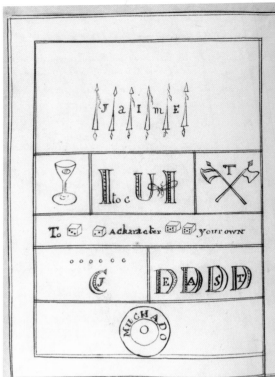
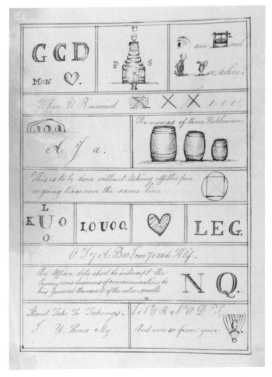
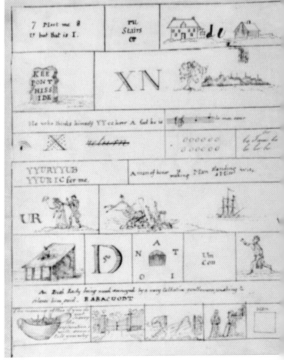

Khan Bund Pass – Boydar Country, 7ᵗʰ March 1857

A faithful friend

'Sheikh Bodeen, Sept 1856'

HILL HOUSE - BAUGHULPOOR -

'Hill House, Baughulpoor', for Margaret Anna Grant [my 4 x great-grandmother] by James Prinsep, 1820

'*Humdrum*' *by James Prinsep, 1823*

'*A Domestic Scene*' *by James Prinsep, 1821*

'About to Start from Benares!' by James Prinsep, 1821

'Making Progress in Chemistry!' by James Prinsep

The Black Castle, Barcaldine, Argyll and Bute.

He lost the middle finger of his right hand in action during the Umbeyla Campaign at Eagle's Nest, Crag Picket on 20 November 1863. As this incapacitated his sword arm, which left him, as an officer defenceless.

The Umbeyla Campaign involved the local Pashtuns of the Yusufzai tribes, who were against Sikh rule, and took place on the border between Afghanistan and the Punjab province of British India (known as the Northwest Frontier since 1901). The Umbeyla Pass was a wild, inhospitable area comprising ranges of steep mountains and, from October to December 1863, the small rocky outcrops of Eagle's Nest and Crag Picket within it were at the centre of the conflict. The landscape of the area could not support a large military unit but, nevertheless, the Pashtuns amassed a considerable force and the British suffered losses approaching 1000 casualties in their attempt to hold on to these two areas.

In a lecture detailing events at Crag Picket given by Major-General Sir Vincent Sharpe KCSI CB RA on Friday, 12 April 1867, he says:

Far left: *Bessie, Alick, Emily, Duncan Campbell.*

Left: *Emily and her brother Alick, Sir Alexander Campbell, 4th Bt.*

Below: *Major-General John Peter William Campbell forefront on the left at Umbeyla Campaign, Crag Picket, November 1863.*

Pencil sketches of Crag Picket by John Peter William Campbell.

Presently Captain Hughes' guns from the position in the rear, threw a couple of shells in the enemy's watch fires, which they at once quitted, and descended in the ravine below. Here they were sheltered from fire of the work, and nothing but a dull murmur told the defenders that a numerous enemy, bent on attack, lay within 80 yards of their slight defences.

Another lecture was presented by Captain Fosbery, VC, of Her Majesty's Bengal Staff Corps, in which he states:

The situation was truly a peculiar one. The small portion of the pass occupied by the forces (about 200 yards in width at that point) and filled with huge rocks in every direction, was dominated on both sides by almost precipitous hills; 1500 feet up, the distance between them was only 800 yards, which give a fair idea of their sharp angle of ascent. From below, the ridges immediately commanding the camp were plainly visible, and on these it was proposed at first to establish outposts, but on reaching these points it was discovered that they in turn were dominated by strong positions further up in the hills, and it thus became necessary to push post after post into the mountains until the process was only stopped at Eagle's Nest, on the left flank and the Crag Picket on the right.

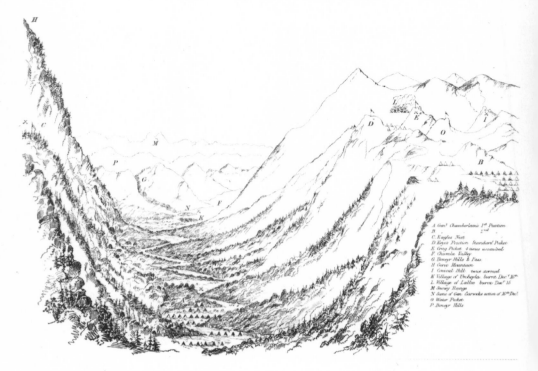

Detailed print of Eagle's Nest, Crag Picket.

I quote from information supplied by the National Army Museum that Colonel George Vincent Fosbery, VC, 1890 'after attending Eton College, Fosbery entered the Bengal Army in 1852. He was awarded the Victoria Cross for his actions on 30 October 1863 during the Umbeyla Campaign whilst a lieutenant in the 4th Regiment of Bengal Native Infantry.'

According to *The London Gazette* of 7 July 1865 it was:

> For the daring and gallant manner in which, on 30 October 1863, when aged about 30 years, and acting as a volunteer at the time, he led a party of his regiment to recapture the Crag Piquet [sic], after its garrison had been driven in by the enemy, on which occasion sixty of them were killed in desperate hand to hand fighting. From the nature of the approach to the top of the Crag, amongst the large rocks, one or two men only could advance at one time.

Above: *J P W Campbell, front row, 2nd from right, 3rd Sikh Punjab Infantry, c. 1862.*

Below: *J P W Campbell, 3rd row centre right, 3rd Sikh Punjab Infantry, 1863, Crag Picket.*

'Whilst I ascended one path,' relates Lieutenant-Colonel Keyes, CB., commanding the 1st Punjab Infantry, 'I directed Lieutenant Fosbery to push up another at the head of a few men. He led this party with great coolness and intrepidity, and was the first man to gain the top of the Crag on his side of the attack.' Subsequently Lieutenant-Colonel Keyes being wounded, Lieutenant Fosbery assembled a party, with which he pursued the routed enemy in the direction of the Lalloo Ridge, inflicting on them further loss and confirming possession of the post.

Major Keyes (front row, on the left), (Sir Charles Patton Keyes, commanding officer of 1st Punjab Infantry), William Boyd Buckle, Political Officer 1840–1872, middle, front row.

View of Abbottabad.

On 29 January 1864, Fanny wrote from Rawalpindi to her brother Sir Alexander Campbell (2nd Baronet of Barcaldine):

My dear brother, I sit down by candlelight to send you a few lines to say dearest Willie is nearly well again, so well I think no more bulletins will be sent to you. He has no use whatever of his right hand yet, but perhaps he will enclose a few lines written with his left. We have been delayed till now for a medical committee, which had to fit in some of the wounded. It assembled today. We only had two hours' notice and Willie, with General Chamberlain [Sir Neville] and Major Keyes [Sir Charles Patton Keyes, known as Keek-Sahib].

Above: *Sketch of Abbottabad.*

Left: *Gravestone of Sir Alexander Campbell, 9th of Barcaldine, 2nd Baronet.*

According to William Wright in *Warriors of the Queen – Fighting Generals of the Victorian Age,* Major Keyes was 'the epitome of the fighting generals who led their men into battle sword in hand'. Fanny's letter to her brother continues:

> His leave expires on the 1st *proximo* so I have been hard at work packing all this day – and our property all starts tomorrow – and ourselves and children the following morning. We hope to reach Abbottabad the evening of the 1st.

> 30 January, 1864 – The medical committee assembled yesterday to decide claims for wounds. Willie was before it and I believe the committee has recommended for a temporary pension, which will be according to rank. Willie, if he gets it, will either receive £200 or £250 per annum for five years. His 'wound pension' of £200 per annum became one for life.

This probably constituted a record holding of such an award, as he held it from 1863 until his death in 1901.

Sometimes fate played a mischievous role. Following the funeral in 1880 of her father Sir Alexander Campbell (9th of Barcaldine, 2nd Baronet) at the Barcaldine family burial ground in the grounds of Ardchattan Priory, Flora wrote to her mother Harriette:

> A dreadful thing happened. Just as MacLachlan was going to read, Uncle Willie, in taking up his place by our side, slipped on the old tombstone and fell right into Papa's grave before Papa's body had been put into it. The pain was great and his ankle was sprained. He lay on his back in the tomb and was got out with some difficulty. He behaved very well.

Mulligatawny Soup

4oz desiccated coconut
2 pints of concentrated stock
2oz ghee
4oz chopped onions
2oz lentils
1 tablespoon curry powder
salt
4 bay leaves
1 small chicken

Make coconut milk by steeping the desiccated coconut in a bowl with ½ pint of boiling water. Leave to become quite cold and rub through a fine sieve to extract the milk. Throw out the coconut pulp.

Cut up the chicken into pieces. Heat the ghee in a saucepan and fry the onions until nice and brown, add the curry powder and fry for a further two to three minutes. Add the chicken pieces and fry, stirring constantly until brown all over. Season with salt. Pour in the coconut milk and simmer for 10 minutes until the chicken is cooked and tender.

Pick out some nice pieces of cooked breast as a garnish and break up the remainder to strengthen the soup.

Heat the stock and add the chicken, onion and curry mixture, the lentils and bay leaves. Boil gently for 2 hours until the lentils are dissolved and the soup quite thick.

Strain the soup before serving. Add the reserved pieces of chicken. Serve with a separate bowl of plain boiled rice and sliced lemon so that the juice may be added if desired to each bowl.

7

ACHIEVEMENTS

Large families were the order of the day and Willie and Fanny had seven children. Their eldest daughter, Emily Frances Margaret (my great-great-grandmother), married her mother's first cousin, Francis Richard Begbie, a union not so unusual in those days, thus doubly linking the two families.

Francis Richard (who produced many pen and ink drawings in the second album) rose to Lieutenant-Colonel and commanded the 2nd Battalion, Prince of Wales Own 2nd Gurkha (Simor) Rifles. He had an exemplary military record which, according to Tony Begbie, was 'filled with tales of derring-do', and for which he was awarded: the India General Service (1854–95) medal, with three clasps; Jowaki Flying Expedition (1877–78); India Medal with Jowaki clasp; Afghan War (1878–80): Capture of Ali Musjid; Afghan Medal with clasp; Mahsud-Waziri Expedition (1881); twice mentioned in Dispatches; Chin-Lushai Expedition (1888–89) with clasp; Chin-Lushai Expedition (1889–90), Chitral Relief Force – Moveable Column (1895), Punjab Frontier (1897–98), Samana (1897), Tirah Expeditionary Force (1897–98) – all of which amount to a pretty impressive chest of medals.

During the Second Boer War (October 1899–May 1902) Francis was mentioned again in despatches after the Battle of the Modder River, which took place on 28 November 1899: 'Maj Lindsay, 75th Battery, gained a painful wound and continued in the command of his battery. Lieutenant Begbie, suddenly placed in command of his battery, led it,

Above left: *Emily Frances Margaret Begbie (née Campbell), my 3 x great-grandmother.*

Above right: *Colonel Francis Richard Begbie, my 3 x great-grandfather.*

and brought it into action with great coolness.' In spite of this illustrious military activity, Francis still found time to be a family man and he and Emily, like her own parents, produced seven children.

Francis's brother Elphinstone Waters had a military record to rival that of his own: he was Ensign of the Madras Infantry, made a colonel in 1859, major-general in 1889 and, keeping it in the family, took over as Brigadier-General of Madras Command in 1895. He was active in the Abyssinian Campaign, the Duffla Expedition, Third Anglo-Burmese War, was awarded a DSO and made Knights Commander of the Order of the Bath. Military accolades apart, Elphinstone was probably best known for inventing the revolutionary Begbie signalling lamp.

'My two cousins', by Francis Richard Begbie.

Far left: *Major-General Elphinstone Waters Begbie.*

Left: *Begbie signalling lamp.*

Below: *Francis Richard Begbie's medals.*

To quote Tony Begbie, '(...)it had a fixed-mirror system, which saw the first operational use of sun-flash signal communication on a military expedition in 1874 (he obtained a US patent on this equipment).' Fuelled with kerosene and with a lens that focused the light over great distances, it enabled the military to transmit messages in Morse code, and was used to great effect during WWI, saving thousands of servicemen's lives.

Of a competitive nature, Elphinstone was the first European to swim across the treacherous waters of the Irrawaddy River, once more proving his extraordinary courage. His actress daughter Kathleen played the part of Flossie Gay in a production of *The Parasites* by Rose Mathews at the Scala Theatre, London in June 1907.

The SAPDD website biographies' section describes Rose as:

> An actress, activist and writer, Mathews' *The Parasites* was presented by the Play Actors as part of a joint bill with Cicely Hamilton's *The Sergeant of Hussars* at the Scala in 1908 to help pay off the costs of establishing the Actors' Association, the forerunner of Actors' Equity. As well as a suffragist, Mathews was a prominent and activist member of the Association, publishing articles, making speeches and serving on the Council of its offshoot company, the Play Actors, alongside Inez Bensusan, Winifred Mayo, and Italia Conti [founder of the stage school of that name]. Her play *The Parasites* aimed to draw attention to the "steamy side of stage life" and the exploitation of actresses by unscrupulous agents. Her one-act play *The Smack* was performed in aid of the Suffrage Atelier [1910].

Kathleen inherited her father's strong personality and clearly must have admired and been influenced by the playwright who, as an active supporter of the women's suffragette movement, ended up in prison at the same time as Mrs Emmeline Pankhurst. For a brief period, my grandmother Esme shared a flat in London with her cousin but was forced to move out when Kathleen died suddenly as a result of slipping in a scalding bath. With the commencement of WWI, Esme, aged seventeen, learned to drive and became a chauffeur living in a garret above the garage. Her job

Above left: *Kathleen and her mother Mary.*

Above right: *Esme at seventeen.*

was to ferry VIPs in a Rolls-Royce to important meetings around London, an occupation which could prove hazardous when the vehicle's narrow wheels were frequently caught in the tramlines.

Emily's brother, Alick, fought in the Afghan War (1878–80) and gained the rank of colonel in the service of the Indian Staff Corps, formerly the 16th Lancers and 15th Hussars. He succeeded as 4th Baronet of Barcaldine in 1900 and it is his simple recipe for fish pie (see page 196) which remains a family favourite today. This is his obituary from the *Bognor Regis Post*, 1931:

DEATH OF SIR A CAMPBELL – ROMANCE OF A BARONETCY

Bognor Regis will hardly be the same without the kindly old gentleman, bearded and wearing a cloth cap, who used to walk the streets, with a word for all, distributing cigarettes, and to the children, largesse in the form of sweets. Probably few of the children were aware that this patriarchal-looking old gentleman was the holder of a well-established

Scottish title, and there were many who were unaware of the romantic story that lay behind his accession to the baronetcy at the age of 78, leaving him with scarcely five years to enjoy this belated honour.

Lieut-Colonel Alexander William Dennistoun Campbell was born in 1848 at Mynpooree, Bengal, his father at the time being an officer in the Indian Army. In 1857, the year before the Mutiny, young Campbell, who was then nine years of age, sailed for England with his mother and was educated at Tonbridge School and Brasenose College, Oxford. In 1871, he was gazetted a sub-lieutenant in the 16th Lancers and later took part in the famous Afghanistan campaign, first with the 15th Hussars, then afterwards with the 17th Bengal Cavalry, being present at Kandahar.

Instead of venturing east, some ancestors sailed to South Africa and Australia, others taking a very different path across the Atlantic to the Americas, amongst whom fought against our old enemies the French. One such intrepid individual was Sir Matthew Baillie Begbie (1819–94) who was born on board ship en route for Mauritius, where he lived until the age of nine before returning to the British Isles, the family settling in the Channel Islands. Educated at Cambridge University he gained a law degree at Lincoln's Inn before entering the diplomatic service and, in 1858, he was appointed the first Chief Justice of the Supreme Court of the wild, undeveloped new Crown colony of British Columbia. In order to reach the remote areas in need of his counsel, generally he travelled on horseback, but sometimes covered hundreds of miles on foot only to find that these primitive outposts lacked acceptable official buildings.

In an account of his life and career, Selwyn Banwell wrote:

> It has been remarked by more than one eye-witness that though Judge Begbie had sometimes to sit in strange circumstances, at unusual times and in incongruous surroundings (he frequently held Court in a log shack or in the open air, in a clearing in the forest, sitting in his saddle as upon a bench of justice), nevertheless the serene dignity and formal air of an English High Court of Justice seemed to pervade the whole proceedings.

Standing at over six feet tall with wild flowing locks and a full set of whiskers in his legal garb, Matthew must have made an impressive sight. An enigmatic individual, not only was he a keen sportsman but also a consummate performer who enjoyed taking part in amateur dramatics and singing in operatic performances. Multi-talented, into the bargain he was an accomplished linguist and spoke more than a dozen Native American Indian languages. Tony Begbie says:

> At the age of 39, Matthew was offered a judgeship, at £800 per annum in faraway British Columbia, Canada. He accepted and arrived there in 1858. BC at that time was a pretty lawless place, much like the Wild West in the US and Begbie soon became the embodiment of law and order. Between his arrival from England and BC's entrance into a Confederation in 1871 he conducted 52 murder trials, handing down a death sentence to 27 of those convicted.

Sir Matthew Baillie Begbie.

This reputation brought about the nickname of the 'hanging judge'.

When gold was first discovered in the colony, Matthew skilfully defused infectious mass rioting, as had been the case in the Gold Rush in the Far West, by controlling the situation with his own brand of careful, wise administration. Tony elaborates:

> He was most certainly the 'terror of the rowdies' and in those faraway gold rush days, there were rowdies aplenty here. Matthew was a firm believer in the swift but fair execution of justice and would sometimes hear cases dressed in his robes while astride a horse. In camp, en route to some mining town, he baked bread and chopped wood and on Sundays

The Palace of Mysore.

would lead singing by the campfire. Hymns, perhaps, and a tot or two besides – one of his first registrars recorded this note after a night spent with Matthew during the journey to another case: 'Glorious fun – drunk, drunk, drunk.' Knighted for his legal work as Chief Justice in this wild frontier, Matthew Baillie Begbie wrote in his will, 'I desire no other monument than a wooden cross be erected on my grave…' But, desire it or not, a monument exists – and a big one, too – snow-capped Mt Begbie, which overlooks the town of Revelstoke, BC [a city on the Columbia River some 400 miles east of Vancouver], was named in his memory.

Pursuing the trend for a career abroad, Emily's brother Richard Hamilton Campbell joined the Madras Civil service and, in 1909, was appointed private secretary to His Highness the Maharaja of Mysore. In a letter to his brother Sir Duncan (5th Baronet of Barcaldine) dated 11 November 1912, Richard writes:

It is a very comfortable appointment. Under ordinary circumstances my life here would be up next year but I have agreed to stay on permanently at His Highness's personal request. Our lives are certainly in pleasant places here and we have a lovely climate and plenty of social activities. Prince and Princess Alexander of Teck [Queen Mary's brother and Princess Alice, Countess of Athlone, the surviving grandchild of Queen Victoria] were here the other day and we found her most charming.

Richard was invested as Companion, Order of the Indian Empire (East India Company) that year (1912) and, true to his word, he remained in the employ of the Maharaja. In a letter to Duncan dated 26 April 1920 from his home, nostalgically named Glenview, in Ootacamund, he writes:

My wife and daughter came back to India last November after a very long absence and we are now spending the hot weather at this lovely hill station, which is the finest in India. We had the Viceroy at Mysore last November and gave him a great show with an elephant *kheddah* camp (an enclosed trap constructed to capture a herd of elephants). Next December the Prince of Wales is coming to Mysore on a short visit. That, too, will be a great occasion. I am in charge of his entertainment and their visit will give me a great deal to do.

When my brothers and I were children Ma would tell us this story about the state visit to India in 1935 of King George V and Queen Mary. Allegedly, the house in which the royal party was due to be billeted had very basic sanitary arrangements and legend has it that 'His' and 'Her' lavatories were installed but not actually plumbed in, each chain fitted with a hidden length of rope linked to two flags on the roof: a red one for the Queen and a blue one for the King. Two servants sat patiently and, as soon as one flag was hoisted, a bucket of water would be hurriedly tipped down the appropriate pipe flushing the cistern below and thus completing the illusion.

PART
TWO

Lemon Cheesecake (Mother's)
[Frances Charlotte Campbell]
– my 3 x great-grandmother

4 chittacks butter
8 eggs
4 chittacks castor sugar
lime/lemon juice and essence to taste

Melt 4 chittacks butter in an enamelled saucepan, whilst mixing
stir into it the well beaten yolks of <u>8</u> and the whites of <u>3</u> eggs and 4
chittacks finely powdered white sugar. When dissolved, add lemon
juice according to taste and a few drops of lemon essence. Line a
pudding dish with butter and bake or cook till thick and keep. If the
mixture oils add beaten up yolk of another egg (without white).

8

NELL'S STORY

The British class system, although less complicated, was almost as rigid as the Indian one, which I look at in more detail in chapter 13. My uncle Roger told me that his 'darling grandmamma [Nell] considered herself to be of the upper ten thousand. Today this viewpoint looks like rampant snobbery but, back then, it was simply how things were. It is possible that the declining wealth of this select echelon exposed their diminishing gentility and engendered regret for glories past – real or assumed – hence the importance of being a "lady" or a "gentleman". As social divisions faded, those not considered to belong to the proper gentleman or lady class were gradually accepted and this led to changes in military and social hierarchy. Promotion to officer from the ranks may have its origins at the time of the Boer War and developed further during WWI.'

Nell was eighteen when she married Alexander 'Alick' Harry Colvin Birch, a soldier sixteen years her senior, on 27 July 1895 in Mussoorie (a hill station north of Delhi in the United Provinces). The wedding was reported shortly afterwards in the newspaper:

On 27th [July] there was a very pretty wedding at Christ Church when Captain A H C Birch RA was married to Miss E Begbie, daughter of Colonel Francis Richard Begbie of the 2nd Gurkhas. The church was decorated with flowers and shrubs were sent up from Dehra [Dehradun]

Above: *Alick, my great-grandfather, with his sister Kate.*

Left: *Eleanor (Nell) Geraldine Birch, my great-grandmother.*

for the occasion, and there was a very large attendance including many officers whose full-dress uniforms lent effect to the scene. The bride arrived at 3 o'clock accompanied by her father and six bridesmaids. The bridegroom was supported by Mr Brandreth of 19th Bengal Lancers. After the ceremony, which was performed by the Chaplain the Rev Mr Langford, a reception was held at the Chapelton, the residence of Col Begbie, and the health of the bride and groom was proposed by General Sir Robert Turner KCH and enthusiastically drunk by the guests. The happy pair left at 8.30 for Cloud End and received the usual tribute of rice and slippers. The gifts were numerous and costly.

The reference to the elegance of the Officers' 'full-dress uniforms' was endorsed when I was drawn as if by a magnet to a stall at a local boot fair. Stacked in a box on the grass was a large volume, *The History of the Dress of the Royal Regiment of Artillery 1625–1897 Compiled and Illustrated by Captain R J MacDonald R A*. In 1877 the Committee of the Royal Artillery Institution obtained the names of certain Officers willing to guarantee the expenses of this project – a 19th century form of crowd funding. However, sufficient monies were not forthcoming and the idea was put on hold until twelve years later when a limited edition of 1500 were printed. I searched through the index and to my delight and surprise saw that not only Alick was a subscriber but was mentioned in a chapter written by General A C Mercer R A. In the paragraph on 'Stocks, etc.' General Mercer states, 'In the beginning of my career, the neck was enveloped in a black velvet stock, into which a padded stuffing was introduced to keep it up; or it was worn over a sufficient accumulation of white muslin, of which one-eighth of an inch in breadth was to border the upper edge of the stock as a finish. In plain clothes, white muslin cravats were then invariably worn, and none but the masters or mates of merchant-men and such-like craft ever dreamed of wearing black.' Apparently, Alick did not conform. General Mercer continues, 'Captain [now Colonel] Birch of the Engineers was an exception, and it is curious to recall in the present day, when all wear black, the vulgarity imparted to his appearance by this departure from the established mode.'

The following year, on 4 March 1896, when she was eight months pregnant with their first child, Nell was travelling in a *tonga* (a horse-drawn carriage) when the animal took fright and bolted, throwing her out of the vehicle. The

The stock in question.

Royal artillery uniform, 1897.

accident provoked a premature birth and the little baby survived only a few hours; the death was announced in *The Pioneer* the following week. Chinese whispers of family history dictated that it was a boy but, in a letter written on 18 September 1913 from her mother Emily to her brother Sir Duncan, it was confirmed otherwise:

> She [Nell] has been unfortunate. Shortly after they were married Capt Birch's battery was ordered on service. I do not fancy there has been any fighting but they are living in tents. He is coming up on three months' leave and there is talk of Nellie going back with him for the cold weather. People can make themselves very comfortable in tents, but I expect she will be the only lady. Poor Nellie. She lost her baby girl; it only lived a few hours.

The little girl was christened Geraldine Cecile. Thirteen months later on 4 April 1897, Nell and Alick had a second child, my grandmother Esme.

The camp.

Alick came from a long-established military family and, after attending the Royal Military Academy in Woolwich, was a gunner in the Royal Artillery. Married for four years, and aged thirty-eight, he was given a brevet promotion from captain to major for his actions at the Siege of Malakand. It is interesting to note that Lieutenant Robert Haldane Rattray, the sole survivor of the *Athol* and who wrote the poem 'The Exile' in 1826, was also present at Malakand.

The poem describes the demise of the ship on which had been sailing for India, which was wrecked off the coast of Africa. Robert was a friend of James Prinsep. There is a possibility that it was his hand that wrote the opening lines of his poem in Margaret Anna's album. This is part of the introduction in the published book of the poem:

The following appeared lately in one of the Hampshire Papers, under the head of 'Naval Intelligence':

In a gale of wind on 29 August last, the *Athol*, a ship of eight hundred tons, bound to the East Indies, was wrecked under Cap Hanglip on the southern coast of Africa, and every soul on board, but one, perished. The Commander of the vessel had two daughters with him, both lovely young women, who were proceeding to a relative in India, where they were to be united to two shipmates, one of whom is the unhappy survivor of the wreck. Baffling variable weather attended them when a tremendous gale set in from the northwest. The ship was thrown on her beam end and the mizzenmast was cut away with the additional loss of her fore topmast and all her boats. After scudding for seven hours the main mast went over the quarter, carrying 12 hands with it. The ship, totally unmanageable, was soon among the breakers and, in a few minutes more, was gone. The sole survivor was discovered on the shore the following morning in a state that excited the liveliest sympathy of those whose timely aid restored him to existence.

In 1897, a fledgling twenty-three-year-old journalist, Winston Churchill, was employed to observe the campaign as war correspondent for *The Daily Telegraph* and, in 1898, a collection of his columns entitled *The*

Story of the Malakand Field Force: An Episode of Frontier War was published. Alick's achievements are mentioned by Churchill:

From the despatch of Maj Gen Sir Bindon Blood, KCB, the Relief of Chakdara August 1897, 'I have the honour to invite the special attention of His Excellency the Commander in Chief in India of the good services of the following officers described above, namely (including) Capt A H C Birch RA.

At Inayat Kila, the General [Jeffreys] and Capt Birch were both wounded, early in the night. The actual casualties were in proportion of the numbers engaged, greater than for any action of the British Army in India for many years. Out of a force, which at no time exceeded 1000 men, nine British officers, four native officers, and 136 soldiers were either killed or wounded. The following officers commanding units and detachments of the Relieving Force are stated by Brigadier-General Meiklejohn [Brig-Gen Sir William Hope Meiklejohn KCB CMG] to have carried out their duties in a thoroughly capable and satisfactory manner, namely Capt A H C Birch RA 8th Bengal Mountain Battery.

In October 1897 Sir Bindon Blood (Despatches, Malakand Field Force) continues:

'(…)in concluding my report I would wish to express my admiration of the fine soldierly qualities exhibited by all ranks of the special force which led into Upper Swat. They fought at Lankakai in a brilliant manner, working over high hills, under a burning sun with the greatest alacrity and showing everywhere the greatest keenness to close with the enemy. They carried out admirable to trying duties necessitated by marching in hot weather with a transport train of more than 2000 mules and they endured with perfect cheerfulness the discomforts of several nights' bivouac in heavy rain. Brig Gen Jeffreys has also described in very favourable terms the gallant and valuable act of Capt A H C Birch RA commanding No 8 Bengal Mountain Battery and his trumpeter Jiwan in rescuing a wounded sepoy of the 35th Sikhs.'

The following information was given to me by Paul Wood of Messrs Morton & Eden Ltd in London (specialist auctioneers of collectors' coins, war medals, orders and decorations, and historic medals), which throws light on my great-grandfather's medals:

> Regarding Lieutenant-Colonel Birch – nice group of medals – his DSO was awarded the New Year's Honours 1918, where he is listed as being on the retired list (he was in his late 50s by that time). Unfortunately, New Year's Honours awards are virtually impossible to research. I would suspect that he was more likely to have been involved in logistics, rather than being involved in front-line fighting. He was commissioned in 1880 and like many R A officers ended up doing Indian Service as the Indian Artillery was disbanded in 1858 following the Mutiny and was entirely staffed by British personnel.
>
> His medals are as follows: India General Service 1854–95, 3 clasps, Burma 1885–87, North East Frontier 1891, Waziristan 1894–95. Second Medal is the India General Service 1895–1902, clasps, Malakand 1897 and Punjab Frontier 1897–98. From 1891 we know that he was serving with No 8 Bengal Mountain Battery during the Northeast Frontier Campaign and he would have served either in the Kohima or the Tanu column (No 8 Battery was split between the two). In the Waziristan campaign, he was part of the 2nd Brigade at Malakand, which took place between 28 July and 2 August 1897.

Alick's medals, the DSO on the left.

*Image from Sketches on Service During the Indian Frontier Campaigns of 1897 by E A P Hobday.
'No 8 Bengal Mountain Battery, under Capt Birch, RA [on horseback], is passing in the
foreground of the sketch'.*

In the preface to his book *Sketches on Service During the Indian Frontier
Campaigns of 1897*, Major Edmund Arthur Ponsonby Hobday writes, 'I
carried a sketchbook with me throughout the operations with which I
was fortunate enough to be connected. The great charm of nearly all
the Campaigns of 1897 has been the fact that our troops were operating
in hill regions hitherto almost unknown and never before traversed by
any British force.' Under his sketch *Looking up the valley, near Ghalegai*
he states, 'Between Ghalegai and Burikot the track runs at the foot of
some fine cliffs, and is probably the remnant of an old Buddhist road,
as it is paved in many places with large stone slabs. A very fine view of
the snows was obtained looking up the valley from the spot where we
breakfasted on this march.'

Paul Wood continues:

Alick was part of the force in the Kotal; one officer and six men from No 8 Mountain Battery were wounded during the Malakand Campaign. During the Punjab Frontier Campaign, 10 June 1897–6 April 1898, he was with No 8 Mountain Battery, as 2nd Brigade Mohmand Field Force. During the Punjab Frontier Campaign, No 8 Mountain battery suffered heavy casualties with one officer and six men killed and one officer and 23 men wounded.

He adds:

Following virtually 13 years of active service, some of it in the tinder box of the Northwest Frontier, he [Alick] was not to see any further service until the Great War by which time he was on the retired list (but still on the reserve) and received the 1914–15 Star, signifying that he had arrived at the Western front prior to the end of 1915.

Alick, third from left, front row, 'Somewhere in France' during WWI.

Regarding the British War and Victory medals, in 1911 he received the Coronation medal (the medal at the end which is detached from it mounting). The other medal is a white metal medal for the proposed Coronation of Edward VIII. These are very common because, as soon as the abdication became apparent, people bought lots of them and held on to them thinking they might become valuable.

When WWI broke out Alick was offered promotion to Brigadier, which he refused, preferring to have an active rather than administrative role the rank would have prevented. Elevated to a full Colonel, Alick was mentioned twice in despatches and was fighting in France in 1915 when his divorce from Nell was heard before the Court. He was awarded the DSO but, although not wanting to spend the money to secure his medal, he was eventually forced to, since he had to attend the ceremony at Buckingham Palace in order to receive it.

In spite of her husband's achievements on the battlefield, Nell found herself locked into a loveless marriage. One day in 1910, when out hunting in Quetta where they were stationed, she met the tall and elegant then Captain Edward 'Ned' Lorimer. Ned was a fine sportsman and good polo player but he never reached the athletic heights of his brother Ian, who played in the finals of the Calcutta Cup – however, he did learn to water ski at the ripe old age of seventy-eight.

Paper chase with the Quetta Hunt.

Colonel Ned Lorimer, my step-great grandfather, painted by his sister Ann in 1906.

In 1901, because of the Second Anglo-Boer War in South Africa (1899–1902), he underwent a protracted nine-month's training instead of the usual two years at Sandhurst Military Academy in England.

When Ned and Nell's relationship became public knowledge Alick filed for divorce citing Nell as the guilty party. In 1914, two years before the separation was finalised Nell, pregnant with Ned's child, fled to Vancouver with her sister Sybill. Ned joined them as soon as he could, after which they left for San Francisco where their son Gerald was born.

On 9 April 1915 Ned and Nell took their year-old baby to New York from whence they set sail for Liverpool on the *Megantic*, of the White Star Dominion Line. This announcement appeared in *The Times, 3 May 1916*:

Probate, Divorce and Admiralty Division.

A Colonel's Divorce Suit.

Birch v Birch and Lorimer.

(Before Mr Justice Bargrave Dean)

[Sir Henry Bargrave Finnelley Deane]

In this undefended divorce case, Alexander Harry Colvin Birch, a lieutenant colonel in the Royal Artillery, now serving in France, prayed for the dissolution of his marriage with Eleanor Geraldine Birch on the grounds of her adultery with Captain Edward Lorimer. Mr Acton Pile appeared for the petitioner: and Mr R J Sutcliffe watched the case on behalf of the respondent and co-respondent. Mr Acton Pile said that the petition and respondent were married on 27 July 1895 and they lived together in India and England. There were two children [Esme and Douglas]. At the end of 1909 the petitioner was posted at Quetta, whither his wife and daughter accompanied him [Douglas remained in England at Osborne House and the Royal Naval College, Dartmouth]. There in 1910, while they were on a riding trip, they met Edward Lorimer, who was a captain in the 17th Lancers [Baluchi Horse]. Later, at the wife's invitation, Captain Lorimer, stayed with the petitioner for a week. Towards the end of 1910 the respondent left for England. The petitioner remained at Quetta until the end of 1913, when he returned to England on leave. Meanwhile the respondent, without his knowledge and against his wishes, had gone to British Columbia. In June 1914, the petitioner received a letter from the respondent dated 17 May from Vancouver Island, in which she confessed that she had committed adultery with Captain Lorimer and said that she intended to live with him as his wife. The petitioner's evidence, which had been taken on *affidavit*, was read. After hearing further evidence, Mr Justice Bargrave Deane pronounced a decree *nisi*, with costs against the co-respondent, and gave the petitioner the custody of the children.

Douglas remained at Dartmouth and Esme furthered her education in Paris at l'Ecole des Violettes. Emily contacted Debrett's (the social reference 'bible' for all British matters from etiquette to marriage), mentioning her daughter's divorce, an act which distressed Nell greatly knowing that this information would be added to the family entry. She and Ned were married in Marylebone, London in March 1917, after which they travelled to India where Ned continued his career with the Royal Indian Service Corps, undertaking many senior administrative duties including trying to keep order after several of Ghandi's so-called 'peaceful' demonstrations had incited riots. Rather than go home on periods of leave, the two of them travelled extensively throughout the country, in a huge Buick from Mysore to Cochin, Bijapur to Calicut, the cave temples at Bhaja, Golconda, Dambal and Hampi in a huge Buick. However, one year, they returned to Europe, holidaying in northern France.

As was the custom, Gerald was despatched to be educated in England and when he had reached his sixteenth birthday, after such a long separation and desperate to see his parents, he borrowed a canoe and

Above left: *Nell in her prime.*

Above right and right: *Gerald.*

Far right: *Sir Henry Bargrave Finnelley Deane.*

paddled solo across the Channel to meet them. He gained a place at Cambridge to read Biochemistry and, like so many students, became an active member of the Communist Party. Historian Richard Baxell records the following passage in his book *Unlikely Warriors: The British in the Spanish Civil War and the Struggle Against Fascism*:

A rally was announced by [Sir Oswald] Mosley to be held at the Albert Hall for 22 March 1936. The response by communists was rapid and widespread. On the day of the demonstration itself, about 10,000 protestors tried to assemble outside the Albert Hall but the area had been cordoned off, all counter-demonstrations within half a mile banned. Around 5,000 protestors reassembled in nearby Thurloe Square, where the crowd was charged, apparently without warning, by police with batons.

Gerald Lorimer Birch described the treatment of an anti-fascist protestor who was arrested and beaten with a baton, solely for protesting about police brutality. According to Birch, the arresting officer repeatedly referred to the anti-fascists as, 'you lot of bastards'. Birch was himself charged with 'insulting words and obstruction of the police' and eventually released, on his own surety, at 2.50 the following morning. (First published by Aurum Press, an imprint of Quarto Publishing Plc. copyright ©)

The *Dundee Evening Telegraph* published this report:

During scenes outside the Albert Hall when a Fascist meeting was being held inside, two defendants were Leslie Kenworthy (45) and Gerald Lorimer Birch (22), a research chemist. Both were charged with using insulting behaviour and Birch was charged with obstruction. Kenworthy was fined 21s [£1.05, approximately £51] and £2.2s [£2.20, approximately £108] costs. Birch was bound over.

When Ned finally retired from the Indian army he and Nell emigrated to New Zealand where his brother Ian had already settled. When Gerald was twenty-three years old he became a member of the International Brigade to fight in the Thälmann Battalion in Spain. At the age of eighteen Esmond Romilly, the nephew of Sir Winston Churchill, was one of the first to volunteer when the Civil War broke out. This is where he met Gerald. In 1937, Esmond wrote a graphic account of his experiences in his book *Boadilla* (Boadilla del Monte, a small town to the west of Madrid) in which he describes my great-uncle as:

> ... a brilliant scientist and Oxford [sic] graduate, sincere and wholehearted communist. His communism was a thing which lasted seven days a week. He had never known hunger, nor oppression, nor fighting. When he reached Barcelona (early in September) Birch was one of the very first members of the Tom Mann Centuria. All the men respected Birch and looked up to him. These men were all communists and all, in one degree or another, came under Birch's influence and recognised Birch's qualities of leadership and organisation.

On the night of 20 December 1936, to the sound of gunfire, Esmond quotes one of their colleagues, Aussie, "'I never saw Birch after that – I called out to him and he didn't hear, just went on as you know, we were all firing, too, so it was the noise, and then I never saw him".' When they reassembled for role call, Esmond writes, 'Birch – no answer, believed killed, *gefallen* (killed in action).'

Gerald was Nell's third child to die. Although Esme used to talk to her children about the 'scandal' and Nell occasionally recounted anecdotes of their time in San Francisco, neither she nor Ned ever talked about their son. When news of Gerald's death filtered through a relative (possibly Nell's sister Charlotte, Aunt Charley) in a letter to Esme, she in turn contacted Ned. Roger, then six years old, remembers his step-grandfather arriving at their house in Nelson, New Zealand and watching him and his mother pacing up and down the driveway, overcome with emotion. He told me, 'Gerald's name and activities were never mentioned in the family. I don't even know if his surname was Lorimer or Birch.' It was, in fact, a combination of the two.

PART
THREE

Princess Royal Custard

8 fresh eggs, separated
1 dessertspoon cornflour
sugar to taste
4 units almonds, blanched, peeled and bruised in a mortar.
2 pints milk

Beat the egg yolks in a deep bowl. Add the cornflour, beating well. Add enough sugar to taste. Add the bruised almonds and pour the mixture into a saucepan. Stir in the milk and put pan on a brisk flame. Stir continuously and once it has come to the boil reduce the flame and stir for a further 15 minutes until thickened.

Fill the custard cups or glasses within half an inch of the top. A quarter of an hour before service, whisk the egg whites, flavouring with essence of almonds or orange flower water during the process. Spoon onto the custard and serve.

9

FOLLOWING IN ROYAL FOOTSTEPS

My great-great-grandfather Francis Begbie's cousin, Gertrude Emma (1842–1924, daughter of Alfred William Begbie and Margaret Watt) married John Master, a retired magistrate from the Indian Colonial Service in Madras. They lived in Montrose House a large, elegant, late seventeenth-century William and Mary mansion in Petersham, Surrey a short distance from the residence of the Duke of York, the future King George V. The two families became close. In a letter to Duncan dated 26 July 1913 Emily writes, 'I must explain a letter from my aunt, Mrs Master (my mother's half-sister) and a great friend of the Queen's.' Gertrude, according to Miranda Carter in her biography of her son Anthony (Anthony Blunt – *His Lives*, Macmillan, 2001) was a dominating woman who 'forced her grandchildren to ingest every last piece of gristle on their plates.'

Her husband John, perhaps a gentler soul, taught the Duke's wife, Princess May of Teck (her title before becoming Queen Mary), to ice skate and, each spring when the first lilies-of-the-valley came into bloom, Gertrude picked bunches of the fragrant flower from her garden and delivered them in person to the young princess. In return for her kindness and companionship, Princess May passed on some of her cast-off gowns to Gertrude and their daughters, and in further recognition of her affection, gifted her a necklace and cross set with Bohemian garnets.

At the age of twenty Gertrude and John's daughter Hilda (1880–1969) – a second cousin of the Earl of Strathmore, father of Elizabeth Bowes-Lyon (mother of our current Queen) – married the Reverend Arthur Stanley Vaughan Blunt, the Anglican vicar of the neighbouring village of Ham. Educated at Harrow and King's College, Cambridge he was approachable, well liked, and an engaging voice in the pulpit. He was also good at games (he played in the North of England Tennis Championships, 1889–91), appreciated music, history, art and travel. Ultimately, he was ordained Bishop of Bradford but must not be confused with his namesake Alfred Blunt, the second Bishop of Bradford, whose vitriolic speech given in December 1936 exacerbated the abdication crisis of Edward VIII.

Hilda and Stanley's second son Anthony was born in Bournemouth in 1907. Educated at Marlborough College, he won a scholarship to Cambridge like his father before him, and it was at university that he became acquainted with Guy Burgess, Kim Philby and Donald Maclean. Anthony joined the Communist Party of Great Britain and was recruited as a Soviet agent to seek out suitable candidates to join the Soviet Union; in 1951, he helped his three companions to defect. Anthony was implicated as a member of this spy network and interviewed many times but without charge. Employed by George VI as Surveyor of the King's Pictures he was knighted for his services and when the King died, he held onto the post until 1972. In 1964, he confessed to being a Soviet spy and, after the news became public in 1979, he was stripped of his honour but never brought to trial. He continued to work at the Palace as Adviser to the Queen's Pictures and

Aunt Gertrude Master (née Begbie).

Drawings. Following a heart attack in 1983

Far left: *Esme, my grandmother.*

Left: *(Sir) Anthony Blunt – Esme's mirror image (image courtesy of the Conway Library, Courtauld Institute of Art).*

Anthony, aged seventy-five, died at his home in Bayswater. By a strange coincidence, having returned from living in France, I was interviewed by Sir Geoffrey de Bellaigue, Surveyor of the Queen's Works of Art to be his personal assistant at Buckingham Palace. Had I been successful, I would have been working alongside my distant relation.

Photographs of Anthony and my grandmother Esme in later years show them to be so similar in looks that they could have been twins.

To my surprise I discovered that, before marrying my grandfather, Cecil, Esme had been engaged to another officer. In a letter to Duncan, Emily writes:

I have also to announce the engagement of my grand-daughter Esme Birch to Captain Dennis Foulkes of the Royal Irish Fusiliers [sic, 3rd Battalion Irish Regiment]. He has been at the front and three times wounded, and is now recovering from these wounds. I fancy the wedding will take place before long.

Above left: *Esme, Roger, Cecil and Sir Malik Ghulam Muhammad, who served as 3rd Governor-General of Pakistan in 1951.*
Above right: *Aunt Charley on her wedding day to Cecil Norton.*

Left: *Brigadier-General Cecil Norton.*

Below: *Their children, Sylvia, Barbara and Phyllis.*

For whatever reason, the marriage didn't happen and, not long afterwards in 1920, Esme married Lieutenant Cecil Trant Shaw, my grandfather.

Cecil contracted malaria in Macedonia and, having been advised not to return to England, was transferred to the 13th Bengal Lancers in the Indian Army. His regimental CO preferred his junior officers to remain bachelors and Cecil, now a married man, was obliged yet again to be moved, this time into the Royal Indian Army Service Corps. Soon after, Nell's sister Charlotte eloped with an officer – another Cecil (Norton) – when she was eighteen years old, much to the relief of her parents who had three other daughters to marry off. The couple had three children: Sylvia, Phyllis and Barbara.

Tragedy struck when Sylvia was accidentally shot by her husband whilst he was cleaning his gun after a hunting trip in Scotland. There was some good news on the horizon, however, when, on 16 January 1916 Emily wrote to Duncan, 'My son-in-law Maj Norton received a DSO in the last Gazette, being mentioned in Despatches in the previous one.'

Uncle Cecil inherited a substantial fortune but lost the lot gambling on the horses and was obliged to retire as Captain and leave India because of his debtors. He hoped to restore his finances by going to South Africa but, when WWI started, his regiment immediately called him up. Returning as a captain and soon promoted to Brigadier he was invalided out after being badly gassed, after which he was never able to sleep lying down, spending the nights upright in an armchair. Since his rank of Brigadier was temporary his pension was that of a captain, which was not enough to make ends meet and, in a letter to Duncan dated 17 February 1922, Emily asks for his help.

> It is hard after his excellent service in the war to have less than a borough dustman in London's job! I fear any chance of being a Knight of Windsor is very distant, as there are no vacancies yet and when there are, they are likely to go by Court interest. The future is not very rosy.

Nevertheless, through Cecil's influential connections he was granted a grace-and-favour apartment opposite St George's Chapel at Windsor

Left: *Lionel Begbie*. Centre: *Florence 'Encie' Begbie*. Right: *Dickie Ray, 'such a bonny boy'*.

Castle where he remained as a Knight of Windsor for the rest of his days. One warm afternoon when he was walking in the grounds of nearby Frogmore House, he overheard the King swearing loudly whilst fishing in the lake, having lost a catch.

Nell's brother Lionel, after going up to Magdalen College, Oxford, entered the Indian Civil Service. Being a magistrate he escaped the dangers of war but instead died of tuberculosis – a disease widespread, particularly amongst less fortunate families – allegedly contracted through the environment of his court. Two of Alick's brothers suffered from this illness whilst being besieged at Ladysmith during the Boer war where one, or possibly both, died. Roger told me that his mother and grandfather caught it and, whilst Nell developed it in both lungs, it appears she was made of stronger stuff and survived.

Nell's sister Florence 'Encie' Begbie married Cyril Ray and they had a son, Dickie. On 18 September 1913 Emily wrote to Duncan:

Encie's baby is such a bonny boy – so good and sturdy and pretty. Everyone falls in love with him. I have never seen a more attractive child, though he is my own grandson!

Esme, so like Lillie Langtry – she had one of those faces.

Sir James Brooke's (Rajah Brooke of Sarawak) cottage.

Above: *Captain Eric Campbell.*

Left: *Sir Duncan Campbell, 10th of Barcaldine, 3rd Baronet.*

Below: *Rose Scott Campbell.*

Encie was less fortunate than Nell and, when Dickie was three years old, she also succumbed to TB, which in her case proved fatal.

Nell's mother Emily liked to maintain contact with relations and connections that consoled her fragile *amour propre*. One was Lillie Langtry, the Jersey-born actress and consort of the Prince of Wales (later Edward VII), whom Esme strongly resembled. She must have had one of those faces. She also spoke of a male forebear who was one of several drawing masters to Queen Victoria who presented him with a green and white ivory chess set for his services.

The following is an extract of a letter from Emily dated 24 July 1913:

> I am anxious to hear Duncan's [Sir Duncan, 3rd Baronet of Barcaldine] opinion about Sir William A [Augustus] Montagu, the Sandwich family. There must have been a previous connection however, between the Montagus and Brookes, as I remember an old letter of Sir James Brooke to my mother [Frances Charlotte] in which he mentioned her mother, Margaret Anna Grant, as being her cousin and her playmate in childhood and, 'one of the sweetest souls that ever breathed'.

On 12 August 1913 Sir Duncan writes to Emily:

> Sir William A [Augustus] Montagu is down as the son of the 5th Earl so I fancy my grandmother [Harriet Montagu] was also the daughter of the Earl. Sir William seems to have been quite persona grata with the Sandwich family and was certainly a gallant suitor. Sir James Brooke wrote to my grandmother about a legacy a lawyer had written about to his sister asking if any descendants of Mrs Grant – Mrs Begbie's mother [Margaret Anna Begbie, née Grant] were living. Sir William claimed my mother as his grand-niece. I think it is pretty clear who Harriet Montagu was. What a queer lot the Sandwich family were!

Reinforcing the link with Sir James Brooke, one of John Peter William and Fanny Campbell's sons, was named Francis James Brooke Campbell (1861–1918). In 1841, at the age of thirty-eight, the title 'Rajah of

Sarawak' was bestowed upon Sir James by the Sultan of Brunei. He reformed the administration, codifying laws and fighting piracy and slavery, both of which were a constant issue during his reign. By a strange coincidence his heir (who gave up the claim to Sarawak) went to live in Wanganui, New Zealand, where Esme lived until she passed away in 1994.

In a letter from Esme dated 1986 she recounts:

> I have just been reading a very interesting book by Elspeth Huxley [whom I once met around a farmhouse kitchen table in Gloucestershire], *Scott of the Antarctic*. As your great-great-grandmother, Emily Frances Campbell, always said that we were related to Scott and I had later been told that it was Lady Scott, not Scott himself, one of whom married a Captain Eric Campbell of Barcaldine.

This was indeed correct; Captain Robert Falcon Scott's elder sister Rose married Eric, Sir Duncan Campbell, the 3rd Baronet's younger brother. Their daughter Erica was born three months after her father's death in Nigeria and, had she been a boy, she would have been the next Campbell of Barcaldine and the family would have carried forward some genes of a true national hero.

Esme continues:

> Sir Duncan Campbell was the head of the Barcaldine branch when I was young and he died in 1926 in a very mysterious way on the way to his club in a taxi or rather, he did not die then but he fell into a trance and never came out of it. It was some time before he was identified at the hospital, though, of course, they would have known him at his club.

PART
FOUR

Potage Bonne Femme

*This soup should have shredded leaves of spinach added at the end.
They will wilt in the hot broth.*

Gather together any amount and kind of beans, lettuce, onion,
carrots, cucumber that are to hand. Peel where necessary and chop
finely. Melt a tablespoon of butter in a saucepan and add all the
vegetables. Sweat for five minutes, stirring every now and then.
Add 1 pint of water and bring to the boil, then reduce heat and
simmer until the vegetables are cooked (about 15 minutes). Push
through a sieve. In a separate saucepan, blend one cupful of cream
with the yolk of an egg. Slowly pour the hot soup onto the cream
and egg, stirring so that the egg doesn't curdle. Return to the heat
and continue cooking for a further two to three minutes. Do not
boil. Season with salt and pepper and serve at once.

10

THE PEN IS MIGHTIER THAN THE SWORD: WRITERS IN THE FAMILY

My 4 x great-grandfather Major-General Peter James Begbie fought against Naning (an area in modern day Malacca in southwest Malaysia, annexed by the British in 1832) from 1831–32 and was subsequently stationed in the Malay Peninsula from 1836–38. A multi-talented and learned man, apart from being a soldier, Peter James was a writer and fine artist. I quote my cousin Tony Begbie:

> Peter used his pen to write about several military campaigns and his
> sketchbook to capture scenes in India and Malaya. *The Malayan Peninsula*
> contains, among other things, an account of the Dutch administration
> in Malacca, a general view of the British rights to Naning and the story
> of the foundation of Singapore – as well as a broad survey of the history
> and customs of the Malays. This scholarly work, printed in 1834, reflects
> the attitudes of early British writers on colonial subjects.

In a gruesome passage from his *History of the Services of the Madras Artillery with a sketch of The Rise of the Power of The East India Company in South India* (1852–53), Peter James writes:

Left: '*Chinese coffin*', drawn by Peter James Begbie.

Centre: '*The church of the Visitation of Our Lady, St Paul's Hill, Malacca*', drawn by Peter James Begbie.

Right: '*View of Penang*', drawn by Peter James Begbie.

Captain Hamilton informs us of a species of *blanketing*, practised in Siam [now Thailand], yet rougher than that experienced by Sancho Panza in the Inn yard. The Siamese method of frightening offenders, without inflicting material bodily injury, is to cause the unhappy criminal to be tossed from one elephant to another who dexterously either receives the body on his tushes (not the points), or catches it with his trunk, and passes it on to another, to the great diversion of the court and every individual except the figurant. Punishments in Siam generally are symbolical of the offences, which have called down the visitation. Thus, a defaulter in the public money is put to death by having either molten gold or silver poured down his throat. Lying, or a breach of confidence, is punished and guarded against for the future by sewing up the mouth, whilst the with-holding of information, on detection, leads to the mouth being slit from ear-to-ear, as an intimation to speak out. A misconception in the execution of orders entails upon the offender a sword-cut over the head, which practice is jocosely called 'pricking the memory'.

Peter James wrote manuals on gunnery and one called *Supernatural Illusions* (1851), a subject that was to become a favourite of Nell, Esme and my mother. In 1856, he moved to the Straits Settlements (a group of British territories in South East Asia established originally in 1826) where, on his retirement in January 1858, he was awarded the title of Honorary Major-General, before returning to England. He died in Clifton, Bristol in 1864.

Harold Begbie (1871–1929) was the son of Mars Hamilton Begbie, brother of Peter James, and my great-great-grandfather Francis Begbie's nephew. Once again, John Peter William was called upon for help. In a letter to Sir Duncan dated 5 February 1896 he writes:

> I enclose a letter from Mrs Hamilton Begbie who is trying to get an appointment as Inspector in the Agricultural Department for her son Harold. Perhaps you would kindly put a good word in for the young man. He is a cousin of my first wife [Frances Charlotte].

Whatever the outcome, Harold became a journalist and prolific author writing more than fifty books on a wide variety of subjects including poetry, political satire, comedy, fiction, science fiction and plays. He was also commissioned to write the Bible stories in Arthur Mee's *The Children's Encyclopedia*, the ten volumes of which my brothers and I delved into with fascination and enthusiasm. Harold was ghostwriter for Sir Ernest Shackleton's memoirs and wrote two political parodies under the pseudonym of Caroline Lewis. Based on Lewis Carroll's *Alice in Wonderland* and *Alice Through the Looking Glass*, they were entitled *Clara in Blunderland* and *Lost in Blunderland* and dealt with the British frustration and anger about the Boer War, criticising the government of the time. His best-known works exposing various political anomalies are written under another pseudonym: Gentleman with a Duster. Harold was a passionate follower of cricket and close friend of Charles Burgess Fry, a politician, writer, diplomat, academic and an outstanding cricketer. Harold penned the poem 'The Proud Cricketer' for *C B Fry's Magazine*, which subsequently appeared in the Manawatu *Evening Standard* in New Zealand on 10 December 1909:

England has played at many a game, and ever her toy was a ball;

But the meadow game with the beautiful name is King and lord of them all,

Cricket is king and lord of them all, thro' the sweet green English shires,

And here's to the bat, and the ball (How's that?), and the heart that never tires.

Oh, glance of the bat, and the dip of the ball, as it hums through the crouching slips

Oh, the buzzing wail of the flying ball and the grin on the bowler's lips;

Oh, the blind, blind swipe and the cut that's caught, and the terribly quick throw-in,

Ah, here's to the wit of the bat (Well hit!) and here's to the ball with a spin.

The soul is glad in the thick of the game, a song through the spirit swims

For the brain is the king of the muscles' swing and lord of the eager limbs;

And it's joy, pure joy, for the hearts of men, the clean, the strong and the sage,

Till the pulse is cold and we're out (Well bowled!) to a flattening lob from Age.

Oh, it's sweet to talk of the summer's eves of the games we have lost and won,

Of the quick-turned wrist, of the shooting twist of the catch and the stolen run,

It's good to show on, (the stinging hand how the hot return was stopped;

And what of my duck, if we lost (Hard luck!) – but what of the catch you dropped?

But when we are puffing through middle life, and it's time for the last sweet knocks,

When our average falls and we fear fast balls, and the young'uns call us crooks;

Well, watching the young'uns play will serve, and still with our latest breath,

'Well played we'll shout from the ropes, 'Not out!' and follow the game till death.

Harold was acquainted with Sir Jesse Boot (the founder of Boots, the Nottingham-based chemist) and during a conversation told Sir Jesse how hard he had found it to amuse and distract one of his children who was recovering after an operation:

I had searched my bookshelves for stories, histories, anthologies, and journeyings. I had carried to the bedside piles of books which I thought the most suitable; and I had read from these books day after day, succeeding for some few minutes at a time to interest the sick child, but ending almost in every case with failure and defeat.

In the same conversation, he quotes Doctor Samuel Johnson (1709–84):

It is worth a thousand pounds a year to have the habit of looking on the bright side of things.

As a result, in 1916 Harold produced a compilation called *Bed-Book of Happiness*. In the introduction, he writes:

If, in my pages, those who suffer find such cheer as warms your heart and lights your mind, glad shall I be but gladder, prouder too, if this my book become a friend like you.

He continued with this rondel:

Beside your bed I come to stay

With magic, more than human skill,

My pages run to do your will,

My covers keep your cares away.

The nurse arrives with laden tray,

The doctor cancels draught and pill,

Beside your bed I come to stay

With magic, more than human skill.

And you thro' faery lands will stray,

At laughter's fountain drink your fill,

For tho' your body cries, "I'm ill!"

Your mind will dance from night to day.

Beside your bed I come to stay

With magic, more than human skill.

At the outset of WWI Harold wrote this patriotic verse, 'Fall In', which was to be set to music to inspire the young and the brave to sign up for the 'War to end all wars':

What will you lack, sonny, what will you lack,

When the girls line up the street

Shouting their love to the lads to come back

From the foe, they rushed to beat?

Will you send a strangled cheer to the sky

And grin till your cheeks are red?

But what will you lack when your mate goes by

With a girl who cuts you dead?

Where will you look, sonny, where will you look,

When your children yet to be?

Clamour to learn of the part you took

In the War that kept men free?

Will you say it was naught to you, if France

Stood up to her foe or bunked?

But where will you look when they give the glance

That tells you they know you funked?

How will you fare, sonny, how will you fare

In the far-off winter night

When you sit by the fire in an old man's chair

And your neighbours talk of the fight?

Will you slink away, as it were from a blow,

Your old head shamed and bent?

Or say – I was not with the first to go,

But I went, thank God, I went?

Why do they call, sonny, why do they call

For men who are brave and strong?

Is it naught to you if your country fall,

And Right is smashed by Wrong?

Is it football still and the picture show,

The pub and the betting odds,

When your brothers stand to the tyrant's blow,

And England's call is Gods!

A portrait of Harold by Walter Stoneman hangs in the National Portrait Gallery, London.

There were other authors in the family, including Esme's uncle by marriage (his wife Kate was Esme's aunt and reputedly the most beautiful girl in India), Sir George Scott Robinson, who was a British agent at Gilgit in the Himalayas from 1890–91. During that period, he travelled on two occasions to Kafiristan in the Hindu Kush, where he was the first European to live amongst the Kafirs, who counted their worth by the number of people they killed. Happily, Sir George avoided that fate and gained additional fame through his role in the Siege of Chitral and, after retiring, he became MP for Bradford where he recorded his experiences in *The Kafirs of the Hindu Kush*.

In the preface, he writes:

In the year 1888, in company with Colonel Durand CB, then a young cavalry captain, I was travelling through the Astor valley of Kashmir to Gilgit. On one memorable occasion, we had made a double march. The track was extremely arduous, and the waning light found us tired and jaded, and still some distance from camp. Silent and slow-footed, we rounded the Doian spur in the gathering darkness, and had begun the descent to the village, when a strange sight to the northwest startled us into open-eyed wonder. Above, the pure sky domed over all, while in front a filmy veil of cloud was suspended, which seemed to magnify and accentuate, instead of dimming, the noble outlines which lay behind. Through this mysterious curtain could be seen a bold curve of the Indus flanked by mighty mountains, and the light yellowish-grey shades of the

Sai Valley, which increased the dream-like unreality. A veritably faery country had been revealed to me.

He was the last person to be made a Knight Commander of the Order of the Star of India, founded by Queen Victoria in 1861; very few were awarded, it being 'at the monarch's pleasure'.

My mother tentatively flexed her own skills with these childish essays, one entitled *The Kite,* penned in India when she was seven years old:

The kite has brown wings, tail and body, and a dark red-brown beak with a tiny bit of a hook. Kites are awful thieves. They often take away toast and bread and any kind of oddment they can find from our houses and they store them in their nests, sometimes with dead rats and parroqueets [sic]. They have got very good eyes and they can see from a distance. In the rainy weather when the white ants come out they swoop down and eat them. Kites are loved by the Indians. It is the rule, if the Indians have a kite, they must always let it go on a Saturday or Friday. The kite's cousin the Brahminy kite has black quills and white feathers and you cannot very easily tell the difference between the Brahminy baby kite and the ordinary kite baby, but if you look hard you will see one has a forked tail and the Brahminy kite has a round tail.

It was once a goldsmith who wanted work, and the rajah got him to work on the verandah of the palace. He hammered a nail in and put a piece of raw meat there every day, and the kite used to swarm down and take the raw meat. And when he had got to be ready with the gold chain he was very sorry that he could not have the gold chain for himself, but he had a brass chain in his box. So, he put the gold chain and the brass chain when he had finished in his chatty [Indian cooking vessel] of gilt and, when the maharajah came for the gold necklace for the maharani, he put out the brass chain and hung it on the nail and the kite swooped down and took it away. And he cried at the king's feat [sic], and said he was sorry the bad kite went and stole the gold chain, when he was quite pleased because he had got the real gold chain in his chatty. The rajah

Esme as a dancing girl with a brass chatty.

gave him the money for the work, and even still more money, because he was so sorry for the gold chain to go the thief kite.

The Indians call their children when they are disobedient and go out in the sun in midday, that they are midday kites. The kite builds its nest with sticks, straw and anything he thinks will make a nice nest. They cover it like a saucer so the eggs can't fall out. If anyone shoots at them or throws stones and an egg falls out, she will get awfully angry and try to take off their topi. A little boy told me that he shot a stone at a nest with a catapult and the kite took off his topi and dropped it, took off his sister's topi and dropped it, and then took off his nanie's [sic] topi and put it on the nest.

Kite and water bearer.

PART
FIVE

Tired Housewife's Cake

1lb flour
½lb butter
½lb sugar
½lb sultanas
½lb currants or other fruits desired
2 small teaspoons baking soda
a little mixed peel
1 teaspoon each of vanilla, almond and lemon extract
1 teaspoon each of grated nutmeg, mixed spice and cinnamon
½ pint boiling milk
2 eggs

Put the soda into the flour, then the butter. Add the sugar and fruit. Beat up the eggs well and add the milk. Then mix all together. Bake 2 hrs in a nice oven. When baked this cake is 5lb in weight.

Left: *Oleander*

Below: *A spring bouquet*

Carnations, by Frances Charlotte Begbie, my 3 x great-grandmother

Variegated geranium

Summer flowers

By Mme Lefevre

Hawthorn

Moss rose, by Eleanor Geraldine Begbie, my great-grandmother

Harebell

11

CHALLENGES FACING THE MEMSAHIBS

[Theatrical] Manager Serlo in Wilhelm Meister [Wilhelm Meister's Apprenticeship, by Goethe] states (we quote from memory) that, '*no man who would wish to cultivate his character, would willingly pass a day without seeing a fine picture, hearing a beautiful piece of music, or letting his gaze rest on the face, and his mind enjoy the conversation of a good and lovely woman*'.

The Calcutta Review, 1856

The phrase 'Anglo-Indian', before it suggested a person of mixed race, was originally used to describe the British living or having been born in India during the time of the Raj, the period of colonial control that lasted from 1858 until Independence in 1947. At the time, countless opportunities arose for ambitious young men to forge successful careers abroad in the Civil Service, the Army, trade and business, many endeavouring to replicate the reassuring British traditions in a foreign country, hoping to secure a bride and start a family.

Encouraged by the chance of an exotic future along with the hope of finding a husband, many single women too gave up a secure environment and sailed into the unknown to India. These brave souls prepared to make the arduous, perilous journey by sea were nicknamed the 'Fishing Fleet', and before the Suez Canal was built, which didn't open until November 1869, the voyage could take six months plus further weeks' travel on land. Not everyone was successful in finding a spouse and, under the soubriquet of 'empty vessels', disconsolate and dejected, they purchased a lonely passage home. Those fresh from Britain who were lucky in the marriage stakes were faced with myriad challenges and it is hard for us to imagine how unprepared they were for what awaited them. Not only did they have to get used to being the wife of a man whom, more than likely, they barely knew, but they had to learn how to run a household in intolerable heat with few, if any, conveniences. Indeed, India could prove fatal for those with more fragile constitutions, and the threat of disease, wild animals, poisonous snakes and biting insects were part of daily existence.

In *The Complete Indian Housekeeper and Cook*, first published in 1888, Flora Annie Steel and Grace Gardiner give advice on how best to cope with some of these pitfalls:

> The mosquitoes are large, venomous and untameable. They bite with as much zeal at the end of the day as at the beginning and have a discriminating eye to open-work stockings.

The Calcutta Review, 1856 states:

> Our fair countrywomen in this trying climate may not always shew [sic] that exquisite soundness of face and form. The divine beauty of the Englishwoman renders her a rival to the finest sculpture of antiquity amid the healthful breezes of her own country. Still, wherever she wanders the charm of expression is never lost, and the refinement and trace of languor lent by this climate are not unfavourable to that source of beauty at any rate. Almost every man in this country may marry: may light up and render happy his home with that loveliness of feature and form, born of loveliness of mind, which shall add the final crown and capital to his moral culture.

Six generations of my family were born in India after brothers Peter and Alfred Begbie, who were my 4 x great-grandfathers, first stepped off the boat in Calcutta at the beginning of the nineteenth century. Many served in the Indian Army and, in the 1800s, it helped to have a certain income to join the Guards since mess and uniform costs often exceeded the salary. Thus, the more adventurous (but less well-off) opted for these postings rather than serve with a British-based regiment. Emily, Lady Clive Bayley and her father Sir Thomas Metcalfe wrote in *The Golden Calm, An English Lady's Life in Moghul Delhi* (1850):

> In the Upper Provinces beer and wine were luxuries which prudent Subaltern officers deny themselves. When people of limited incomes do not choose to meet at tea and spend the evening cheerfully together, invitations must necessarily be restricted, and can only occur at long intervals. These 'station dinners', as they are called in large cantonments, are only given by persons who can afford them.

In a letter (courtesy Tony Begbie) sent from India to his brother Alfred (my 4 x great-grandfather), Elphinstone Begbie writes:

> You get off wonderfully with 17 shillings a week for wages. Our servants come to ten pounds and ten shillings exactly a month, although we do not keep a trap. It is a fallacy to say that India is cheap. The climate in the hills is delightful and we live comfortably, but not economically. The rates and taxes in Ootacamund come to 18% of the annual rental.

Conditions on the cantonments (permanent residential structures associated with a fort) situated in remote, strategic parts of the country where these adventurers lived whilst on campaign, were basic in the extreme. Emma Roberts writes in *Scenes and Characteristics of Hindostan, with Sketches of Anglo-Indian Society* (published in three volumes in 1835):

> The cantonments in the neighbourhood of Etawah region [in Uttar Pradesh] are particularly desolate, and exhibit in full perfection the

Above left: *A cantonment.*

Above right: *Mughal Koht, Balochistan fort, Northwest Frontier.*

Camp Sheikh Bodeen, 1856.

Captain Browne's house.

dreary features of a jungle station. Upon a wide sandy plain, nearly destitute of trees, half a dozen habitable bungalows lie scattered, intermixed with the ruins of others built for the accommodation of a larger garrison than is now considered necessary for the security of the place, a single wing of a regiment of *sepoys* being deemed sufficient for the performance of duties of this melancholy outpost.

The cantonment popular at Sheikh Badin in the district of Paniala in what is now Pakistan was created by the British in 1860 as their summer headquarters. In *The Highlands of India* (1882) Major-General D J F Newall describes it as, 'about 35 miles north of the frontier station of Dera Ismael Khan (affectionately known as Dehra Dismal) and 25 miles west of the nearest point of the Indus lies Shaikh Bodeen Sir [sic], the highest point of a remarkable range of hills bordering one side of the fertile plains of Murrie'.

Captain Campbell's house (my 3 x great-grandfather).

In 1864, the Deputy Commissioner Major Urmston confirmed the pleasant environment:

> There are no two opinions as to the healthiness of the sanatorium. It has been proved beyond doubt to be a most valuable place of resort for officers and families on the frontier during the hottest months of the year; and, after the experience of two seasons, I can safely affirm that, though its outward appearance is less attractive than other hill stations, its beneficial effects upon the constitution, especially of ladies and children, are very great. The cool breeze, which sets towards sunset is very refreshing, and dense fogs and clouds are rare.

Ethel, married to another of John Peter William's sons, Francis James Brooke Campbell, wrote to Harriette Campbell (J P W's sister-in-law) on 22 June 1896 from the cantonment in Allahabad in Mussoorie that there are:

...a good many military, any amount of civilians, barristers and missionaries. It is the HQ of the Northwest Provinces. The Lieutenant Governor is there, too, and it's a huge native city.

Emma Roberts describes bungalows that had been 'improved' by adding doors and windows:

The bungalows are not in their primitive state, for upon the first occupation of these remote jungles, doors and windows were not considered necessary. A 'jaump', or frame of bamboo covered with grass, answering the purpose of both – are still sufficiently rude to startle persons who have acquired their notions of India from descriptions of the city of Palaces. Heavy, ill-glazed doors smeared over with coarse paint, secure the interiors from the inclemencies of the cold, hot and rainy seasons.

'Dabble dabble', drawn by Emily Campbell, my great-great grandmother before she married Francis Richard Begbie.

The walls are mean and bare, and where attempts are made to colour them, the daubing of inexperienced workmen is more offensive to the eye than common whitewash. The fastenings of the doors leading to the different apartments, if there be any, are of the rudest description, and the small portion of wood employed is rough, unseasoned and continually requiring repair.

There were none of the luxuries we take for granted today. Even by the time my mother was born in 1922 bathrooms were not a place to linger, being equipped solely with a simple tin tub set in a depression in a concrete floor wide and deep enough to take the waste. Water, heated across the compound in the kitchen outbuilding some distance from the main house, had to be transported by their servants in four-gallon kerosene cans. Ma dreaded bath days, not only because of the contact of rough carbolic soap but because the cool, damp atmosphere of the washroom lured snakes in from the garden via the drain.

Then there was the invisible but very audible presence of beasts roaming outside at night. Emma warns that

'If the doors be left open at night, moveable lattice-styled jaffrys [shutters] must be substituted to keep out the wolves and hyenas which take the liberty of perambulating through the verandahs and the gardens are the haunt of the porcupine and panthers in the ravines.'

Indoors was no safer a haven:

'The chopper or thatch of a bungalow affords commodious harbour for vermin of every description. Squirrels, rats, with an occasional snake or two, form the population of the roof and are comparatively quiet tenants. These intruders are only divided from the human inhabitants of the bungalow by a cloth, stretched across the top of each room from wall to wall and secured by tapes. This cloth forms a ceiling and shuts out the unsightly rafters of the huge barn above...'

Wildlife abounded.

A typical dwelling.

'Where is he? Where is he?' by James Prinsep, 1820, depicting the interior of a budgerow, a slow passenger boat used on the Ganges.

Prior to cloth being used, snakes would often drop from the bamboos onto the sleeping family below – but the cloth itself was only a temporary solution. Emma confirms:

It proves a frail and insufficient barrier; the surface yields with the pressure of the vermin showing distinctly the outlines of the various feet. When it becomes a little worn, legs are frequently seen protruding through some aperture and as the tapes are apt to give way during the rains, there is a chance of the undesired appearance of some hunted animal, which in its anxiety to escape its pursuers, falls through a yawning rent into the abyss below.

Uncle Roger remembers clearly trying to sleep under such uncomfortable – and for a small child – terrifying conditions. Emma also mentions the insect noise:

> At nightfall, a concert usually commences in which the treble is sustained by the crickets, the bass is croaked forth by innumerable toads. The bugle horns of the mosquitoes are drowned in the dissonance and the gurgling accompaniment of the musk rats are scarcely to be distinguished.

Sleep would be further disrupted by 'the yells of a wandering troop of jackals'. It was enough to floor the doughtiest of new arrivals from safe, sedate old England. Thus, in an attempt at achieving a 'peaceful' night, beds were positioned in the centre of a room, the feet standing in bowls of water raised to a considerable height off the floor to prevent ants from climbing up. Anti-mosquito curtains made from fine nets would be attached tightly, forming a barrier, but the occupants could still hear the scratching and scuttling of lizards and other horrors in the rafters overhead.

During the hot, humid, airless summer months many of the European residents decamped to hillside homes. Wives and children escaped the stultifying heat of the plains by departing to their houses built at several thousand feet above sea level where the climate was pleasant and healthier, although this brought another set of problems.

'The hot winds season with all its miserable tedium and confinement is not healthy and such places as Agra and Meerut are considered favourable to European life, as far as actual disease goes.' – *The Calcutta Review,* 1856.

Flora and Grace had particular advice for women setting up their summer residence, which had scant accommodation for servants:

> When securing a house, inquire as to the number of servants' houses, and stalls for ponies and cows, and limit the number of your followers as far as possible. Do not be alarmed at the dirty state of the house at the beginning of the season – it is English people's dirt, not entirely natives – and arises simply from the fact that at the close of the previous season

the fair occupier could not or would not take the trouble to leave the house in decent order before descending to the plains. The house should therefore be thoroughly cleansed, chimneys swept, floors scrubbed, and all carpets and hangings put out in the air. Throw open all doors and windows, examine them for broken panes of glass and light blazing fires. The tapes should be taken off the bedsteads and washed; sanitary arrangements should be minutely inspected. Next, go around your house outside and have all rank vegetation cut down – it harbours dirt and emits injurious gases, which taint the air. In a cholera epidemic, the neglect of such precautions may prove fatal for it has been well said, 'Cholera is a dirt disease, carried by dirty people to dirty places from dirty places.'

To stay on the plains where fierce winds blew from March to May meant immense physical discomfort, so residents devised their own, eco-friendly form of air conditioning.

Emma Roberts writes:

The tatties are put up – thick mats of the roots of a fragrant grass [fescue] upon bamboo frames, fitting into the doors and windows, all the apertures in a contrary direction being closely shut. The tatties are kept constantly wet by men employed to throw water upon them on the outside and the wind which comes through them is changed into a rush of cold air, so cold sometimes as to oblige the party within to put on additional clothing. The atmosphere is scarcely bearable: excessive and continual thirst, languor of the most painful nature, and irritability produced by the prickly heat, render existence almost insupportable. Every article of furniture is burning to touch: the hardest wood, if not well covered with blankets, will split with a report like that of a pistol, and linen taken from the drawers appears as if just removed from a kitchen fire. The nights are terrible every apartment being heated to excess. Gentlemen usually have their beds placed in the verandahs, or on the *chubutoor* [a limed, terraced area] and they incur little risk in sleeping in the open air at a season in which no dew falls and there is scarcely any variation in temperature.

Flora and Grace say that '*punkahs* [a large, swinging fan made to function by a servant called a *punkah wallah*] are used from 15 March to 1 November and for day and night work three are required.'

In her letter to Harriette, Ethel writes:

> The heat has been terrible in the plains – 120 degrees in the shade at Allahabad. The nights are the worst time. We can hardly sleep. The rainy season is very near now, and when that begins, the great heat is over.

Before leaving Rangoon for Bangalore Eric Campbell (who would become the 6th Baronet) wrote to his uncle Duncan:

> The monsoon is breaking up and we are beginning to enjoy fine weather again. The sunsets here are magnificent just at present. The commonest animals about here are bullocks – horses don't thrive in this country. The bungalow swarms with rats. Once the soothing rains returned, life became more tolerable but this was heralded by violent winds and tornadoes, the air between storms sultry.

Cattle at rest.

Futtypoor Sicree, 1892.

'The tatties were discarded and the fresh, cooler air brings instant relief,' writes Emma R, 'all life begins to spring back into action and the grass can almost be seen to be growing green again'.

But with the frequent changes in temperature came the increased risk of catching malaria, which rose up from the marshlands, she continues:

Fever and aigue [ague] are the common complaints, the former is often fatal and the utmost vigilance is requisite to avoid the danger to which both natives and Europeans are continually exposed,' warns Emma, adding that the bungalows often suffered in the wet season when, 'the pillars of the verandahs sink and lose their perpendicular and out-offices and servants' houses are frequently washed away.

The Calcutta Review, 1856 relates:

Physical exhaustion is not the worst, there have been instances of men who, by imitating the more natural habits of the people of the country, have preserved their vigor to a great degree. A temperate diet stimulating the senses rather by spices than alcohol, regular habits, and all the air and exercise consistent with comfort, may carry a person of good constitution with comparative impunity through his Indian career. Still, the waste of life is great and few who have gone through 30 years of this country, and an adoption of a native mode of life, which is agreeable neither to our pride, our prejudices or our previous training if he is a man at 50 is neither likely to live very long nor greatly enjoy life in his own country.

Watercolour of a swamp scene.

Lemon Barley Water

4 large units pearl barley
8 lumps of sugar
the rind of 2 lemons and if liked, a little of the juice
1 quart of boiling water

Put the barley in a saucepan with water to cover it. Bring it to the boil then let it boil for 5 minutes. Next strain off the water and <u>throw it away.</u> (By doing this you remove the slightly bitter flavour of the barley, and improve both the colour and the flavour of the barley water.) Next put the barley in a jug with the thinly pared rind of the lemons and the sugar. Pour on the boiling water. Cover the jug tightly and leave it until cold, then strain off the liquid into a clean jug and serve as cold as possible.

12

WHILING AWAY
THE TIME

We took our buggy (for the horse had long been sent to his stables on account of the sun), and hurry home. It is nearly eight in the morning and it is already necessary to close the house. We have now ten or eleven hours before us of complete confinement. In England at this time of the year we should have every exhibition open from the Vernon Gallery to the Crystal Palace; the thronging streets, the fragrant meadows, the river, the racecourse, the cricket-field. Look on the reverse: a couch is backed with matting so as not to provoke undue perspiration. One room (influenced by the thermantidote[5]) is habitable, enjoying a temperature of 90 degrees Fahrenheit. There we will lie extended and read till breakfast time. If we are military men we shall see the *havildar* (sergeant) of our Company and look over the order book. A careful housekeeper will order the roughest possible sketch of a breakfast and dinner. Dressing supervenes the cold bath, either plunge, shower or with earthen vessels full dashed over the glowing frame, imparts at least a temporary vigor. We prolong breakfast as long as we possibly can, say till eleven. We shall probably now again undress and, lying extended in some

5 A rotating wheel fixed into a window and encased in wet tatties (screens made from fibrous grasses) which help to cool and circulate the air.

darkened room, one of Mr Routledge's shilling volumes in hand, sleep till noon, that meal for which we have not much appetite, the iced beer however is grateful. Nothing more remains, from three to six, but more novels and more sleep.

At the latter hour, we dress again and go forth in the buggy for a languid drive through the evening air. Conceive the scene: trees white with dust, bending before the tempest of furnace wind, miserable deserted looking bungalows, compounds surrounded with broken mud walls, languid natives in bed outside their doors in the villages, used-up dogs sleeping in the street and, as it grows darker, the skulking form of a wolf or jackal trotting across the road in search of prey in the form of a cow or native child. On our return once more to the hated bungalow or the scarcely less odious Mess House, chairs are ordered into the verandah where, under the unequivocal relief of a large hand-punka, we sit till summoned to dinner. Dinner ensues in due time with its horrible steam and sparkle. It is a wonder if some of the guests be not asleep before the removal of the cloth and so more time is killed till nine o'clock. Cheroots are lighted the instant the cloth has been withdrawn and an adjournment to the billiard room shortly after follows for all those who can dispense with the eternal punkah. Now a feeble pool, a few mild bets, a conversation which, in the total lack of topics sometimes too ribald for description, prolong the weary evening until we retire to our own house to spend a hot and sleepless night before rising to a similar seventeen hours of dullness on the morrow.

The Calcutta Review, 1856

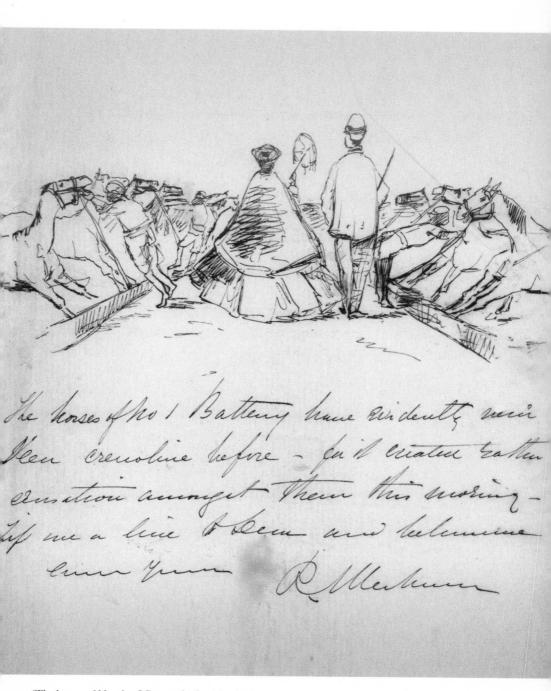

'The horses of Number I Battery had evidently never seen crinoline before…'

A variable climate, tradition and social etiquette in India exposed many problems for European women and how to dress presented a constant problem and, with little to occupy their free time on the compounds, the women and children had to make their own entertainment. Emily, Lady Clive Bayley and her father Sir Thomas Metcalfe describe how things were in *The Golden Calm – An English Lady's Life in Moghul Delhi*, (1850):

> There is little scope for feminine industry. Charity bazaars, which put so many fair fingers in motion in Europe, are almost unknown in Calcutta. Where there is (the prospect of) no theatre, no fancy ball... dresses and decorations to be fashioned out of such materials as only a bold and imaginative spirit would consider applicable. The climate in India is, unfortunately, adverse to needlework or any work whose beauty may be endangered by hands, which cannot be kept at a proper temperature. Thread to netting [taking the precaution to use silver implements[6]] is the employment best adapted to hot weather, but the fair proportions of many a scarf have been curtailed by the want of a few reels of cotton.

The following passage is an extract from Lewis Carroll's novel *Sylvie and Bruno Concluded*, in which the character *Mein Herr* sums up perfectly the attitude from the male perspective at the time:

> Mein Herr took up Lady Muriel's work, and examined it through his large spectacles. 'Hemming pocket handkerchiefs?' he said, musingly. 'So that is what the English miladies occupy themselves with, is it?' 'It is the one accomplishment,' I said, 'in which Man has not yet rivalled woman!'

On fashion, Emily Bayley says:

> A great deal of amusement may be derived from the varieties of costume and manners displayed by the arrivals from Europe and Calcutta. Where two ladies are dancing *vis-a-vis* in some quadrille, there will be

---

6 Silver implements (needles and pins), unlike those made from steel, do not rust.

a difference of at least ten yards in the skirts of their gowns... A few wardrobes of India are actual curiosities.

Going out without a hat was something that was never done.

'When the great heat of the sun has to be braved, a large pith hat should be worn, a real mushroom, that will protect the nape of the neck,' write Flora and Grace.

Clothing naturally had to be adapted to cope with these extremes of temperature.

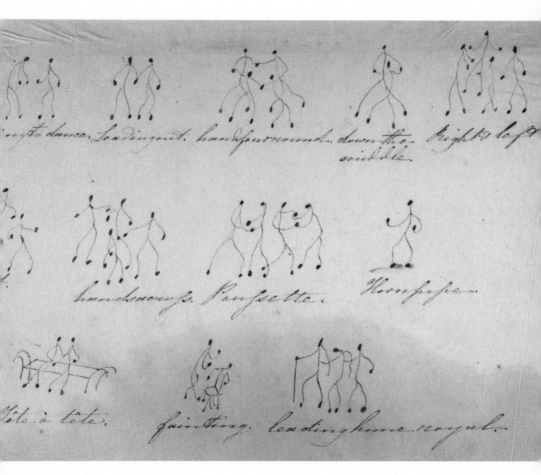

'At the dance'.

Nell and Esme in their giant mushroom hats.

Above left: *Nell and Esme trying to keep cool.*

Above right: *Esme (top middle) having fun.*

Nothing is cooler or more wholesome during the Indian hot weather than soft washing silk, and its use does away with the necessity for flannel, which is so irritating to some skins. The great secret of coolness and comfort, however, lies in wearing one well-fitting, absorbent under-garment, and one only. For this purpose, nothing can be better than a combination garment of silk or cellular flannel, with the lower part made loose and roomy, without any knickerbocker frills and furbelows.

And for extreme hot weather night attire, they advise, 'nothing is pleasanter to wear than fine nun's-veiling.'

When I was sorting through one of the cupboards after Ma died, I found a bolt of this cream-coloured fabric. It must have been well over 150 years old but it was still in immaculate condition. Emily continues, 'To have them (nightgowns) with short, open sleeves and low at the throat sounds cooler than it is in reality, and gives mosquitoes and sand flies a larger area for exploration.'

Esme and my great-grandmother Nell dealt with the heat in their inimitable way: neither ever wore knickers.

Shops in the army compounds did not exist and everyone relied on visiting vendors. Usually itinerants from the Far East, commonly known as 'John Chinaman', they arrived by bicycle or on foot, laden with panniers filled with hand-embroidered silk and crêpe de chine underwear, lace-trimmed nightdresses, tablecloths, linen and other fripperies. To this day, I continue to use antique family napery and I wore some of Nell's silk nighties and camisoles until they fell apart with age – or when I could no longer fit into them. Amongst her wedding gifts was a beautifully embroidered cushion. Handmade in China, it was covered in flowers and intricate patterns exquisitely worked in coloured silk and gold threads. Rather than use it for its intended purpose, Nell had it skilfully cut into several pieces, which were then appliqued onto a black, silk-velvet jacket and, for an avid bridge player, it was perfect for chillier evenings when playing cards.

This is how a typical day in the hot season should be spent, according to Emma Roberts:

Rise at five o'clock after a night spent under a thermantidote or on the roof with a *punkah*. Take tea and toast. Then, on some pretence or another – if possible with an object – stay out of doors riding, driving or walking till half past seven or eight o'clock. Take some porridge and milk or some other light refreshment, remembering that in the hot weather it is a mistake either to feel empty or to take a full meal. Then bathe, either in a swimming bath or in a tub full of really hot water. Look after the housekeeping either before or after your bath. Not later than ten o'clock, breakfast, and work steadily at something till noon. From twelve till two lie down and read or sleep. It is a horrible mistake to sleep after a heavy luncheon; you wake unfit even for your own society. Lunch at two, or half past. Work till four, bathe, dress and go out. Dinner at eight.

The club became the pivotal centre of social life, and competitive sporting activities thrived. Horses were not only a means of transport – depending on the terrain, racecourses and polo grounds were carved out of the landscape. Nell rode daily and hunted with the Quetta hounds in the pursuit of jackals – not foxes – accompanied by her friend Roberta 'Bertie' Wyatt. Both women smoked and Bertie broke social etiquette by lighting up in public, swiftly followed, I shouldn't wonder, by Nell. Ahead of her time, Bertie was reputedly the first woman in India to abandon the sidesaddle in favour of riding astride, an action regarded as nothing less than scandalous. This clearly remained a topic of fierce debate a generation later because Esme, aged fourteen, wrote the following about her friend:

Joyce is such a little silly about riding astride but I don't mind because she knows nothing about either way, because she has walked on a pony both sidesaddle and astride. She says sidesaddle is the best. First of all, I tried arguing with her, but that was no use, so now I say, 'Have you trotted both ways? Have you cantered both ways? Have you galloped both ways? Have you jumped both ways?' She says 'no' and tries to go on talking, but I chip in then, 'I don't see what you know about either way.'

Left: *Between chukkas.* Centre: *Quetta races.* Right: *Quetta polo ground, 1903.*

Each family employed at least one *syce* (groom) to care for the horses. The *sahibs* [the title given to European men] were often too busy to keep an eye on the stables and it was up to the *memsahib*, the lady of the house, to make sure that they were well run and the horses kept in good condition. Flora and Grace suggest that:

> It will, in the authors' opinion, be invariably found a good plan to limit the number of servants employed in the stable as much as possible. If one grass-cutter be given to each horse, one syce to every three horses will, as a rule, be found sufficient. Every morning after breakfast he [the syce] will come for orders, and again after dinner at night; since, if a horse is to be taken out early in the morning, a good syce will wish to know it, in order that he may arrange that the animal gets its feed in good time.

Emma confirms that:

> A camp-dinner for a hunting party is not only an exhilarating but a very interesting meal. The most elaborate picnic provided for a *fête champêtre* in England, where people are put to all sorts of inconveniences and must content themselves with a cold collation, is nothing to the luxurious displays of cookery performed in the open-air in India. Under the shelter of some brushwood, the spits turn merrily and rapidly over charcoal fires.

Mrs Roberta 'Bertie' Wyatt.

An oven is constructed for the baking departments, and all the beneficial effect of hot hearths for stews and other savoury compounds are produced with the greatest of ease and facility. All that can be attainable within the range of fifty or sixty miles is brought into the camp upon the heads of coolies, glad to earn a few *pice* [paisa] for their daily bread.

With plenty of time on their hands the men played polo, cricket, golf and went pig-sticking (hunting wild boar), while the women joined their husbands on the golf course, learned archery, played bridge, painted, sketched and rode. They learned how to handle a gun, many becoming crack shots, which provided them with vital protection should they find themselves in a perilous situation.

In 1988 Esme wrote to me saying:

I have generations of forebears sent out to India, most of them also born there and many dying there and if Grannie [Nell] and Bertie [Wyatt] and their partners were playing golf, we had armed sepoys stationed on the surrounding hills.

Above left: *A game of cricket, Kohat 1862.*

Above right: *Pig-sticking (hunting wild boar).*

Flora and Grace describe how,

The great feature of Indian society is, of course, the daily tennis party, where, in large stations, costumes suitable for garden fêtes are worn, and even in small ones a dowdy dress is the exception. For those who play tennis, at least two really smart costumes are necessary, and in addition two white flannel skirts to be worn with various bodices. Indeed, for young girls nothing is so becoming for tennis as the plain skirt and loose bodice, smocked perhaps with some dainty colour, with a broad sash to match.

ARGUMENTUM AD HOMINEM.

Bessie. "Now, don't you like this much better than Rackets, & a lot of stupid gentlemen?"

[Ofcourse he does." Who wouldn't?"]

Above right: 'A lesson in archery', sketch drawn by Francis Richard Begbie.

Above: *Nell and Bertie Wyatt on the putting green.*

Far left: *Dressed for the game.*

Left: *Game, set and match.*

Below: *Spectators enjoying the tennis.*

Ghee

Melt one pound of the best unsalted butter you can find – the better the butter, the better the ghee. This will give you approximately ¾lb of ghee. Break up 1lb butter and put into a saucepan with 2 bay leaves and a few cloves. Bring to the boil, the water will evaporate and the butter will separate, leaving sediment on the bottom of the pan. Continue boiling (but do not stir) until the clear butter stops making a noise and the sediment begins to take on a light brown colour. This may take a little more than 15 minutes. Remove from the heat and allow to cool a little, but whilst still hot, pass through a sieve lined with a fine muslin cloth. Pour into sterilised jars, cover and keep in a cool place. Once cold the ghee will turn hard and is an opaque yellow. It will last indefinitely.

13

DEALING WITH THE SERVANTS

The Indian caste system became increasingly rigid under British rule. At the top of this hierarchical pyramid are the Varnas (Brahmins): the priests and teachers. Second in line come the Kshatriyas: the rulers and warriors. Thirdly are the Vaishyas: merchants and cultivators. Last in line are the Shudras or servants, amongst whom are the Untouchables, or Dalits who were given the menial tasks.

Most British residents in India understood that domestic harmony demanded tact and diplomacy. Help for the lady of the house was offered again by Flora and Grace in *The Complete Indian Housekeeper and Cook*:

> The duties of mistress and servants, the general management of the house and practical recipes for cooking in all its tranches. Perhaps the best advice the authors can give to any one going out to India is this – Life is uncertain – more uncertain, if not as to duration, at any rate as to circumstance, in India than elsewhere. Therefore, look six months ahead and no more.

Sketch of an Indian soldier.

Fanny Charlotte Begbie (my 3 x great-grandmother) was born in Banda, Bengal and, when she married John Peter William Campbell in 1847, long before Flora and Grace's domestic bible was written, she was told: 'Be sure to tell the servant in charge of washing dishes that a plate has two sides.'

Grace and Flora mention that some *memsahibs* had learned it was better to steer clear of the kitchen, 'for the simple reason that their appetite for breakfast might be marred by seeing the *khitmutgar* (butler) using his toes as an efficient toast-rack (fact); or their desire for dinner weakened by seeing the soup strained through a greasy *pugri* [head wrap]. Even supposing the kitchen is kept in a cleanly state, it by no means follows that the food will be cooked cleanly, and the mistress must always be on her guard against the dirty habits which are ingrained in the native cook. The strictest morning parade will not prevent him stirring the eggs into a rice pudding with his finger.'

The first meal of the day comes in for particular criticism:

Breakfasts in India are for the most part horrible meals, being hybrids between the English and the French fashions. Then the ordinary Indian cook has not an idea for breakfast beyond chops, steaks, fried fish and quail; a menu rendered still less inviting by a khitmutgar at a side table, toast and butter coming in when the meal is half-finished and the laying of the table for lunch while the breakfast eaters are still seated, combine to make newcomers open their eyes to Indian barbarities.

My grandparents amused themselves with a ritual whereby one member of the family would take a knife and press it hard onto the pat of butter to see how much water could be squeezed out, a cunning ploy occasionally used by the vendor to increase its weight, thus extracting a greater profit.

The indomitable duo of Grace and Flora add:

A good cook is not made, he is born; so if you are lucky enough to find one, do anything to keep him – short of letting him know that you are

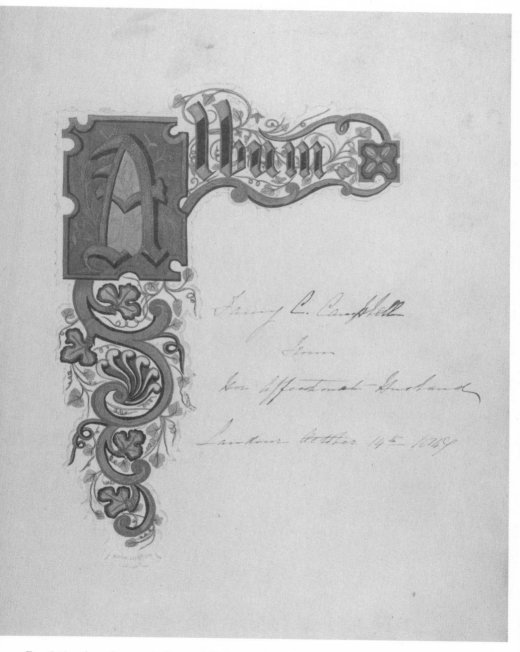

Frontispiece from the second album, a gift from John Peter William Campbell to Frances (Fanny) on their wedding day.

anxious to do so. Finally, if in the hot weather the results of his hands are poorer than usual, and he shows a captious dislike to criticism, give him a blue pill [anti-bilious pill], or present him with a bottle of Eno's Fruit Salts. It is very bilious work stooping over a hot fire with the thermometer above 100 degrees.

My grandparents employed around ten servants who lived with their families on the compound – standard even for an officer of modest rank and paid for out of his own purse. It sounds grand but this was perfectly normal and my grandparents needed several syces to care for Roger's donkey, Fairy, Ma's pony and their own horses.

Left: *The family's servants, Roger on the far right.*

Below: *Ma on her pony with the syce.*

Sometimes the bearer and *khitmutgar* became long-time retainers and developed close personal ties, along with the cook who travelled with the family whenever they moved. Those employed by my grandparents remained in contact with them long after they left India for New Zealand, even to the extent of exchanging presents.

This charming letter to Esme (in which Roger is referred to as Raja Sahib) is from their gardener Ali Shah in Campbellpur, clearly missing the family after they emigrated to New Zealand in 1936. It is obvious from his letter that Ali Shah was very fond of the family and, aware of his limitations, dictated his letter to a scribe. I have copied it verbatim to retain its charm:

Roger, bear and bearer in Thandiani. Roger was frightened by the outcrops of rock, believing them to be crocodiles.

'Campbellpur Cantt: 15/6/1936
Respected Madam,

I was extremely delighted to receive your kind note of 15th ultimo, for which I am particularly thankful to you for remembering your poor Mali. No sooner I received your letter a thought instantaneously struck to my mind and I found as if I actually standing in service in your presence on hearing my voice in the compound while I was attending to your bearer soon Raja Sahib came out he was astonished to see me and remarked.

Raja Sahib: Salaam Sallam.

How you arrived here Sarda Ali.

Sardar Ali: I became very fond of you therefore I arrived here.

Raja Sahib goes inside and informs Mammi of my arrival.

Mammi: Where is he.

Raja Sahib: He is out in the garden.

Mammi: Let us go out.

Esme.

Mammi is surprised to see him and remarks: Hallow – Sardar Ali. Are you well.

Was Sahib alright. How is the garden at Campbellpur.

Sardar Ali: Sahib is going on alright, and the garden is flourishing and is abundant of flowers, especially the scenery of yourself planted candiful as admirable. After about a month of your departure, your small beautiful garden rose to fill blossom and the visitors were very much pleased to see its delightful scenery.

Raja Sahib: How is my garden.

Sardar Ali: Your tomatoes are of very nice species. Garden yields about a pound daily. Double Jasman is giving good flowers and the roses are also nice dues. Whoever comes in the rest house he is overjoyed to see your splendid pretty garden.

Miss Sahib: How is my cat.

Sardar Ali: Your cat is well and has 3 offspring one gentleman boys, and 2 gentleman ladies. I am trying to send you their photos as soon as a Camera is available. The names of 3 offsprings are, as follows:

Miss Gooseberry. 2. Miss Strawberry (name proposed as mama's self-planted. Strawberry is in abundance). 3. Double Jasman.

Raja Sahib: How is your small pony.

Sardar Ali: It was happy and sends you his greetings, and is now trained to make 'salaam' with his legs.

As soon as I finished above statement, I was surprised to find myself there in your presence although I was here. Sahib has promised to afford me the facilities of being trained as a bearer, when I hope I may have the good luck of reaching in your presence. I hope you will be pleased to send me a view plan of your residence in Newzealand [sic], if possible along with the members of the building.

With best wishes, I remain your poor Mali, Sardar Ali Shah,
c/o Major Shaw, Bungalow No. 37, Camel Corps, Campbellpur, Cantonement [sic].

The servants were keen to impress their employers. Emma Roberts writes:

Pen and ink drawing by Francis Richard Begbie, 1869.

The *khitmutgars* who wait at table will stir the tea for their master and cut up the meat upon their plates, if permitted to show their diligence by such minute attentions.

Running a large staff could lead to misunderstanding. Flora and Grace encouraged the new arrivals to learn to speak a little Hindustani in order to be able to give clear, intelligible orders to their servants:

A good mistress in India will try to set a good example to her servants in routine, method, and tidiness. Half an hour after breakfast should be sufficient for the whole arrangements for the day. Never do work which an ordinarily good servant ought to be able to do. If the one you have will not or cannot do it, get another one who can.

When Esme, Ma and Roger joined Nell and Ned in New Zealand, Esme and Nell amused themselves by speaking in Hindustani when in public.

They warn that however good a servant…

The best of them will, if put to it, give a final polish to your teacup with some portion of his own clothing, or place fresh-made mustard on top of old to save the trouble of cleaning out the pot.

Clearly, Flora and Grace expected their readers to conform to their exacting standards, but I admit to being guilty on occasion of the latter charge.

Vegetable Curry

Vegetable curries may be varied indefinitely.

1lb potatoes
1lb peas
1 small cauliflower
1 unit curry powder
2oz ghee
2oz onions, chopped
1 teaspoonful salt
½ pint water.

Peel and cut the potatoes into quarters and the cauliflower into neat pieces. Heat the ghee and fry half the quantity of onions till brown, stir in the curry powder, frying it well with the onions. In a couple of minutes add the water and salt. Bring to the boil then add the vegetables with the remainder of the onions. Cover the pan and simmer for an hour. There should be little or no gravy.

14

FEEDING THE FAMILY AND THE IMPORTANCE OF A VEGETABLE GARDEN

All these things may be done in this country: we may get watercolour pictures, we may accumulate prints, we may decorate our interior with tasteful furniture or, if we are rich, with artistic statues and tasteful ornaments. There may be flowers under the tatties or all sorts in the veranda for the great heats only last two months and then, when the rains have once begun, the flowers may be put out into the veranda altogether. Many annuals may be sown towards the end of the hot weather. Hedges may meanwhile be kept in order. The trees be looked to and the summer house kept in repair and beautified: creepers grown, terraces of masonry with steps and rough vases erected to break the monotony of the surface (one of the minor evils of many parts of India); furnishing a pleasant, natural, innocent and healthful occupation, connecting us with home and with the great men of the past, many of whom have loved a garden.

The Calcutta Review, 1856

During the nineteenth and early twentieth centuries elegant dwellings with black and white faux Tudor facades reminiscent of Surrey sprang up in the cooler hill stations and were given names like *Fernside* or *Greenwood* (two examples of my family's summer residences), comforting reminders of the Home Counties. Shimla, situated at 7238 feet in the Himalayan foothills, was a bustling city with its churches, bazaar and theatre, and became the preferred summer capital of the British. In 1906 the Kalka to Shimla railway, was constructed making the area more accessible.

Quetta, the capital of Balochistan, was the Indian Administration headquarters. A fertile area situated at over 5500 feet above sea level, it was known as 'the fruit garden of Pakistan', perfect for the cultivation of almonds, cherries, apples, pomegranates, pears, plums, peaches and apricots – even vines, which thrived in the valleys. A major military station, Quetta commanded a vitally important strategic position in the Northwest Frontier and from there families would take trips to visit other places of interest such as Ziarat ('shrine' in Hindi), a snow-covered mountain resort over 8000 feet above sea level northeast of the capital. Unfortunately, this natural paradise was frequently disrupted by unpredictable earthquakes. There were other dangers. Once, when my mother travelled with Esme, through the Khyber Pass near the Afghan border in 1936, she could remember seeing the sun glisten on snipers' guns up the hillside; if anyone needed to answer the call of nature, you were advised never to stray away from the vehicle.

These high-altitude hill stations were refreshingly comfortable during the day, but nights could be chilly, with snow remaining on higher ground, which explains why many of the recipes are for hearty stews and steamed puddings. Reliable Emma Roberts writes:

> Climate all over India, even in Bengal (where Darjeeling developed as
> a hill station), is delightful from October to March – all is brightness
> and beauty outside the house; summer gardens glow with a myriad of

One of the summer residences.

Shimla, 1862.

flowers, native and exotic, while within fires, especially in the evening, are acceptable and blankets are necessary to ward off the inclemencies of the night.

Gardens were created with seeds sent from home: foxgloves, roses, honeysuckle, harebells, convolvulus, anemones, hawthorn and pinks were lovingly tended and thrived – even grape vines were trained over pergolas. Emma Roberts writes:

The gardens afford a more agreeable method of passing the short period of daylight, which the climate will permit to be spent in the open air. They are large and well planted but the *mallees*, or *malis* [gardeners], are extremely ignorant of the European methods of cultivation.

In the larger hill stations, there were 'Sweet lemons, limes, oranges and citrons offer, in addition to their superb blossoms and delicious perfume, fruit of the finest quality,' says Emma, who praised the state of Bengal in eastern India for its fertility, both in the availability of meat such as deer, wild boar, hares, partridge, duck, geese, quail and peacock, and for the finest prawns.

A balcony bedecked with vines.

The malis at work.

All varieties of vegetables were sown, including artichokes, asparagus, beans, root crops, cabbages, potatoes, tomatoes, lettuce and cucumbers, some of which did particularly well. According to Emma:

> The seeds of European vegetables are sown after the rain season [from mid-June to mid-October] and come to perfection during the cold weather: green peas, cauliflowers and cos lettuce appear at Christmas sustaining, without injury, night-frosts which kill them in their native climes. The hardy plants – celery, beetroot and carrots – never attain their proper size and are frequently deficient in their flavour. Common poultry are also found in an untamed state: they go under the denomination of jungle fowl and are quite equal to any feathered game which is brought to the table.

Like her predecessors, Esme enjoyed gardening from a young age and, as a small child, was given her own plot. In a letter sent from England to her parents she asks:

A pretty verandah.

How is my garden getting on, please? Do use any lettuce that is big enough and if my radishes – the black ones – are ready, please use them, too.

The growing of onions and aubergines was apparently best left to the *mali*, but the pricking-out of vegetable and flower seedlings should be overseen since, 'the mali believes his thumb to be all-sufficient for planting; whilst the addition of a forefinger provides him with the best of trowels.'

Emma continues that:

Nothing makes an Indian house look so home-like and cheerful as a verandah full of blossoming plants and hung with baskets of ferns. There, it seems to the writer the garden is not merely a convenience or a pleasure, it is a duty.

Practical Handbook to the Kitchen in India, 1891 explains the layout of the kitchen:

The kitchen should be roomy, light and airy, with contrivances in the shape of shelves and other conveniences, for laying out in order all utensils and other necessaries inseparable from the kitchen. The oven and all the fireplaces should be constructed of firebricks, and not of the ordinary clay bricks so generally used in Indian kitchens, requiring constant repairs, to the great annoyance of the cook and hindrance to his work. A good supply of reservoirs or large earthen jars (*jallahs*) for fresh water is essential. Of these there should be two at least, both to contain equally good clean water, but yet to be applied to two widely different purposes – the one for washing, and the other exclusively for cooking the victuals. Those who can afford the expense ought to have a reservoir on the terrace of the kitchen, and the water brought down by means of a pipe, with cock attached; which would effectually prevent dirty and greasy hands being put into the reservoirs. The drainage should be well constructed, with a sufficient incline to carry away easily all washings and offal; and the doors and windows provided with finely made bamboo chicks, to keep out the flies, which at some seasons are more troublesome than at others.

Great cleanliness is necessary throughout the kitchen; the flooring as well as the ceiling, the walls, and every nook and corner, ought to be kept constantly in familiar acquaintance with the whisk, and the knight of the broom called in occasionally to aid the cook in the work of a thorough turnover. There are very many kitchens in India the ceilings of which are cleaned only once in three years, when the triennial repairs to the premises oblige it to be done. The very best recipes, however, for ensuring a perfectly clean kitchen, well-tinned utensils, and fresh water, are the frequent visits of the lord and lady of the mansion to the cook. On these occasions, expressions of satisfaction should never be withheld, if deserved, at the mode of cooking or serving up, where not merited, the one or more instances should be particularized and such modification as may appear necessary be gradually suggested.

Attention should next be directed to the order and cleanliness of the kitchen: let there be no sparing of praise, if well-deserved – such treatment is encouraging; and then, if need be, anything disorderly or unclean can be pointed out more as a passing remark than as one of complaint or censure. Finally, one other suggestion is of no little importance, *viz*, cats, dogs and sweepers, as a rule have no business in the kitchen. The sweeper, or, as he is elsewhere called, the 'knight of the broom', should only be admitted either before the operations of the day have commenced, or after their final termination. Ninety-nine sweepers out of a hundred know that intrusions in the kitchen are against all established rule throughout the length and breadth of India. And yet, if the master or mistress be indifferent, not only the knight, but his lady also will indulge their fingers in many a savoury pie.

It is no uncommon thing to find them constantly in kitchens of houses of gentlemen ignorant of the rule, peeling potatoes, shelling peas, and performing other offices for the cook, in expectation of some return for such assistance or service rendered. Never quarrel with a good cook if his only fault that of eating from your kitchen; all cooks will do so, and a good one will eat no more than a bad one. The cook should be kept well supplied with dusters, of the commonest kind, for cleaning and wiping pots and pans, and two dozen of a better, yet coarse description, for straining soups, &c. There ought always to be a supply of twine for tying up roast meats, &c.

A quarterly reckoning should be taken of all the kitchen property in charge of the cook; this is more particularly necessary in houses where there are frequent changes of cooks and servants. The articles of rice, sugar, ghee [clarified butter for cooking], curry condiments, poultry, salt and other non-perishable articles are procurable all the year round, and may be purchased at all times of the day or night; but it is not so with meat, fish, and game, or with fruit and vegetables; there are seasons for these, and when in season, if not procured betimes in the morning, the chances are ten to one that all the arrangements for that day's meals will be sadly disorganized.

Another inconvenience experienced by some families(occurs when) ordering a particular description of fish or vegetable, which is really not in season. The order is frequently misunderstood by the servant, who procures an article widely different from that ordered, or he returns empty-handed, with the declaration of the truth, '*piah neigh*', or '*millah neigh*', which means, 'could not get' or 'could not find'. In order, therefore, to obviate these disappointments and inconveniences, it is deemed desirable to give a list of such articles of consumption as are procurable monthly in the Calcutta daily markets before proceeding further with other matters.

Rice is consumed by most European families at breakfast, tiffin, and dinner. It is eaten at breakfast with fried meat, fish, omelette, country captain, or some other curried dish, and, being invariably followed by toast and eggs, jams, fruit &c., one *coonkee*, which contains about as much as an ordinary breakfast cup, or say half a pound, will always be ample for four tolerably hearty consumers.

Flora and Grace state that:

> One often sees three table servants waiting on two people, while the whole cleansing work of a large, dusty, dilapidated Indian bungalow is left to one man, who is also scavenger, dog man, poultry man, and general scapegoat. The authors' advice therefore, is – Cut down the table servants and increase the sweepers.

On a more practical note, insofar as kitchen requirements were concerned, Emma Roberts writes:

> There is no regular supply of European articles at Etawah [in the western part of Uttar Pradesh, bordering Rajasthan]; the residents are not sufficiently numerous to encourage a native to traffic in beer, wine, brandy, cheese and so on. These things, together with tea and coffee, several kinds of spices, English pickles, and English sauces must be procured from Cawnpore [a city in Northern India on the River Ganges, southeast of Delhi]. Everything in fact belonging to the wardrobe must be procured at Cawnpore, the metropolis of the Upper Provinces. A crash of glass or crockery cannot be repaired without recourse to the same emporium, excepting now and then, when an ambulatory magazine makes its appearance, or the 'dandies' belonging to boats which have ascended the Ganges from Calcutta, hawk about small investments, which they have either stolen, or purchased for almost nothing at an auction. On these occasions, excellent bargains are procured: boxes of eau-de-cologne, containing six bottles being sold for a rupee, and anchovy-paste, mushroom-ketchup etc. at less than the retail price in England.

I came across this nostalgic letter from a Mrs K Warwick in an edition of *Home and Kitchen, the Magazine of the Brown and Poulson Cookery Club*, dated October 1938:

> I thought you might like to hear of my little experience in India long ago in 1912. I was living in Quetta, and like every young wife always trying

to get something nice to cook for my husband. Well, one morning early I went to the Kitchener Market to see what I could get, for I always did my own shopping and cooking. I was just at the last shop in the Bazaar, when up on a corner shelf I saw a yellow packet and what should it be but dear old Brown & Polson Corn Flour! Well, I shall never forget my joy at finding a shop where I could get good English things. I told my neighbours and we used to have little parties to see who could make the nicest cakes. Those were really happy days!

Part of the household.

PART
SIX

Emily Campbell's Christmas Cake
(my great-great grandmother)

1lb butter or ½ margarine/½ butter
1lb currants
1lb sultanas or: 3¼lb fruit: ¼ almonds
1lb raisins
¼lb mixed peel
¼lb almonds
4 breakfast cups of flour
2 heaped teaspoons baking powder
1 teaspoon cinnamon
½ teaspoon ground cloves
1 teaspoon mixed spice
½ teaspoon ground nutmeg
1 teaspoon each of vanilla, almond and lemon essence
1 wine glass of brandy (or wine)
10 eggs
1lb brown sugar

It was typical of Emily not to include a method. One can
assume that all the ingredients are combined and then placed
in the oven until cooked.

15

ESME AND DOUGLAS

Esme was born in 1897 in Dehradun, followed by Douglas in 1900. When he was about six, Douglas was sent to England to board at Mount House Preparatory School in Plymouth, Devon. I have many of his letters from those years and they tell the story of a little boy desperate to be with his family. It is hard to imagine the loneliness he must have felt, separated by thousands of miles from the place where he had been born and spending all his holidays either at school or farmed out to friends and relations, although he wouldn't have been the only boy to do so.

During his years at school, Douglas wrote ceaselessly to his parents and sister Esme, addressing most of the envelopes thus: Mrs. Birch, c/o Col. Birch, Quetta, India. What a successful postal service it must have been in those days.

He would write stories to entertain them, this one (mistakes retained) penned when he was eight:

> As many storys say about the Boar war, but not this one! It happened at the beginning of the war, that a man called Sir Robert had to leed the Mountain Artillery up the side of a mountain out in Africa. Now it happend that Sir Robert was a bit of a funk. When he heard what he had to do a thrill of horror ran down his back. At Mess a man called Jones said to him, 'Well, Robert, how do you like leading the Artillery up the mountain side to fight the Boars.'

Emily in her senior years.

Left: *My great-great-grandfather Francis Richard with Esme, Nell and Douglas.*

Below: *Douglas, Nell and Esme.*

Douglas, the future mid-shipman.

'I do not mind,' he said but they knew he lied. As morning dawned, Robert awoke to find the Genarell shaking him and saying, 'Wake up, wake up, Robert'. He got up and had breakfast and filled his knapsack with food, and called the Artillery together and started off.

When he was eleven the school had a visit from polar explorer Ernest Shackleton, which Douglas found fascinating. He wrote:

A lot of boys went to Shackleton's lecture. Lt Shackleton braught [sic] a motor car to drag the sledge and he had a gramophone, which made the penguins look uncommonly sick.

Douglas's parents returned to England rarely and he saw them perhaps when on leave once in two years at the most. He missed his mama particularly.

> My dear Mummie,
>
> There is an assault at arms on the 8th of July. It is a great time for parents to come down. I have got enough money to pay for your ticket if you would like to come. It is going to be awful fun as there is a tug o' war for each term. If you would like to come down I will ask my servant where you could stay the night if you liked. If you can't come please write and tell me and I will ask Esme, that is if you can't come. Please don't come if you don't want to, Douglas.

In another letter to his parents in Quetta, Douglas tells of a forthcoming 'jym' display, obviously upset that he would be without family support.

> All the boys, uncle's sister's [sic] and mothers, fathers and friends are all going to be invited. I hope you like being on board. I hope this letter will catch you on the way out. I have looked out on the shipping card when you arrive and it said on the 22nd and Miss James says if it arrives before that, will you write? Please will you say who I am to go to for the holiday?

This obviously was of huge concern to Douglas because he sends a second poignant letter a few days later in much the same vein:

> I trace your course on the way out on my new atlas. I heard that you arrived at Suiz [sic] the day before yesterday and that you arrived in Port Said. I am going to give Daddy a electric lamp to frighten away noxsious [sic] insects that ought to be trodden on. If I pass the navy exam when I resign will I get an old age pension, please?

The fear of not seeing his parents from one year to the next persists. In 1910, when he was nine, he wrote:

Father Christmas arriving on a camel.

Please couldn't you tell me whenabouts you are coming home at all. I want to you my collection of cigarette cards. I have got a good many. I have been collecting Arms and Armour for a little over a week, and I only want 8 more for the set which I will soon get I hope. When I give up collecting I will send them out to you to look at. I have one of the best collections in the school.

I am going to play my very best cricket and see if I can be moved up in the second eleven. Please, <u>when</u> are you coming home? You know the aunt you said was coming home in Febuary [sic] she hasn't come yet and it's May but I don't mind much because it is very nice here. I have not got very much more to say, but please tell me who I am going to go to for the holidays? Am I to stay here [at the preparatory school] or not as you have given no definite proposal.

So many of his letters mention their visits to England, which were inevitably delayed. Always caring and wanting to please, Douglas seemed to be the kindest-natured child in spite of minimal contact with his family. When he was ten he wrote:

Please tell me if you can, when Esme or any of you are coming home, so that I might be able to collect some presants [sic] for the person who is. I can draw trains much better now. I got a letter from Dennis this morning. I heard from him that you arrived today. Please write and ask Mrs Cox to tell Miss James that I am not allowed to eat fat for I have to, and Miss James won't believe me when I say I am not. I have just got the set of foreign maps and the set of English maps. Please, what is that unknown aunt called, and has she got a boy? You said she would come in February and it is long past that now. I wish I was out in India. I would love to see that mongoose you had. Was your tortoise a big one and does it walk fast? Ours is called Messipitamia [sic].

In a letter to Esme he asks:

Do sheep really have black noses as it put in that postcard of a Baluchi shepherd? P.S. Could you send me some Indian something because I have not had a parcel (not counting Xmas and birthday) for over 1½ years, if it's not to [sic] much trouble. I sometimes feel rather lonely at night. I know a lovely bit of rhyme. It is about *One more river to Jorden* [sic]. I will only say the first part because you know the rest.

'The animals went in one by one, the elephant chewing a chelsey [sic] bun.
The animals went in two by two, the elephant and the kangaroo.
The animals went in three by three, the elephant riding the back of the flea.

The animals went in four by four, the fat hipopatimus [sic] stuck in the door.

The animals went in five by five, the bees wer [sic] lucky they went in a hive.

The animals went in six by six, the elephant got in a terrible fix.

The animals went in seven by seven, the duck thought he was waddling to heaven.

The animals went in eight by eight, the tortoise thought he was going to be late.

The animals went in nine by nine (I don't know how to spell this so I will spell it

disgustingly), the ginepig sat on the porcupine.

The animals went in twenty by twenty, Joshia [sic] said to Noah, that's plenty

So the ark was sold and rotted away, and was made into matches by Bryant & May.'

Not to be outdone on the poetry front, Esme wrote to Douglas in October 1912:

Read with attention the remarkable piece of poetry that follows... Evening Standard says: 'Miss Belvoir has a truly remarkable insight into the pathos of a microbe's life, and expresses herself fluently and rhythmically, etc. etc.'

A MICROBE TRAGEDY

He was a bug and she was a flea,

And both were happy as microbes be.

In their snug little nest in the sleeve of my vest,

Alas! Alas! Poor bug! Poor flea!

One day to his flea said the kindly young bug,

'I'm going exploring' and with a last hug he departed.

She is now broken-hearted.

Alas! Alas! Poor bug! Poor flea!

He never returned to his poor little wife.

When I felt him exploring I ended his life.

To the wash went the flea in my v-e-s-t.

Alas! Alas! Poor bug! Poor flea!

Esme includes a second poem:

'THE FLEAS' WOOING'

O marry me, o marry me, you dainty little flea,

I will to you be so true, sweetest little flea.

O do be mine, O please be mine,

O lovely little flea.

The maiden blushed,

To her he rushed and kissed her pashnotlee [sic].

'You really love me, so' she cried,

That timid little flea.

'Let's married be, and then you'll see,'

Replied he joyfully.

PS She married him and was of course disillusioned, but that is the fate of all

who marry fleas and otherwise.

Meat Roasted in a Saucepan

Meat cooked in a pan on the fire retains its juices and is very tender. Any type of meat can be cooked in this manner as well as poultry. Potatoes roasted with the meat are very nice and put them in ¾ hour before the end of cooking the meat.

Put 2oz butter or good dripping in a pan large enough to take the piece of meat or chicken. Dredge the meat with salt, pepper and flour rubbing in all over. Brown meat in fat. No water is needed if the meat is fat, but poultry and lean meat will need extra butter and ¼ pint of hot water added when the meat is browned.

Put on the cover and shake the pan constantly to prevent burning. Simmer quietly, basting and moving it about frequently in the pan till cooked thoroughly. Make gravy in normal way. I would suggest draining off any excess fat, stir in a tablespoon of flour into the juices before adding some vegetable stock or boiling water. Bring to the boil and simmer for a minute or two to thicken. There will be no need for further seasoning.

16

DANGEROUS JOURNEYS AND OTHER HAZARDS

The children who remained in India with their parents (mostly young girls, as their education was considered to be less important) were sometimes faced with situations of which they had little, if any, experience. When she was thirteen, Esme wrote to her parents during a journey she was making to Ziarat from Quetta. As well as being known as the fruit garden of Pakistan, this area boasted the largest juniper forests in the world, some specimens allegedly over five thousand years old. The soft climate offered respite in the heat of the summer and generally was approached first by train, then on horseback or horse driven carts. It was also a major military hill station, commanding a vitally important, strategic position in the south in Balochistan. Her letters start with the news of her travels:

8 July 1910. We had such an awful journey up. First of all, it was alright [sic] on the train and quite cool but very soon it got awfully hot and there was nothing to do. We got out at *Katchh* [Kutch] and waited half an hour on a boiling platform whilst Colonel P trotted about and talked. Then he got the luggage over to the other side, then we waited twenty minutes whilst he got everything piled up on the cart, then we got into the *tum-tum* [a carriage drawn by one or more horses to carry people or cargo] and drove to the *dak* bungalow [used for transferring post and

accommodating travellers, particularly government officials] where we had a meal called 'breakfast'. It consisted of hard-boiled eggs, oranges, bread and butter and *dak* bungalow tea and condensed milk. It tasted simply poisonous and I am sure it was. Then we did a fifteen-mile drive behind a particularly unpleasant smelling pony and a man who whipped the wretched beast every other minute. At one place, we got out and walked up a steep hill; that wasn't so bad but every time we thought we had come to top we found we had not.

When at length we arrived at Khan *Dak* Bungalow we had tea with exactly the same things to eat only this time I could not stick the tea so I drank water. [The water in Ziarat comes from mountain springs and is exceptionally good and health giving.] It was so cold that I had to put my rug around me and so had Joyce. Then we had dinner which was exactly the same things we had had for breakfast and tea except that we also had a leg of cold mutton and some stewed fruit.

Esme at Kutch station on the way to Ziarat.

Anemones and lily-of-the-valley by Frances Charlotte Begbie, May 13, 1844

Left: *Bluebell*

Above: *'Le 2 Mai,
1843' by Mme
Lefèvre*

Left: *Anemones*

Flowers the sole luxury which Nature knew,
In Eden's pure and guiltless garden grew.
Gay without toil, and lovely without art,
They spring to cheer the sense and glad the heart.

Left: *Scented geranium*

Below: *By Eleanor [Nell] Geraldine Begbie, my great-grandmother, May 15, 1844*

In pleasure's dream or sorrow's hour,

In crowded hall or lonely bower,

The business of my life shall be,

For ever, to remember thee!

Sophia LITTLE.

A poem from a friend

Campanula

By Eleanor Geraldine Begbie, February 1843

Delphinium

Two days later, on 10 July 1910, Esme writes:

Everything is better now and I am getting used to it. The tea and milk and boiled water and the rest is pretty vile but I suppose in time I shan't mind. The day before yesterday we went for a walk for the first time because it has been

A dak bungalow.

raining as steadily as possible and we only just got back before the rain came down really heavily. We went first of all round camp paths and had a look at the Residency [built in 1892 originally as a sanatorium, it was where the founder of Pakistan, Quaid-e-Azam (1876–1948) spent the last days of his life. It then became the summer residence of Government officials and is now a national monument], which has some very nice trees. Then we came down the path and went up a very steep road, the Magi Road, and had a look at another road that leads to Prospect Point. [Prospect Point is about four miles from Ziarat and has breath-taking views of the Koshik valley].

I was dead tired and awfully thirsty as all the time I had been here I had not once had a proper drink and have not yet. But still we went on and at last in dessperation [sic] I sucked raindrops off a juniper tree. It was not very nice but it was better than nothing. Then we got home I gulped down a glass of water. We went for a walk this morning. 2½ miles about, one mile going was good walking then we turned up a *tangi* [a gorge or gulley].

But then the tone of Esme's letter takes a disturbing turn.

When we got on again I sat in front as three behind was rather hard luck on the pony and Col P put his arm around me again and again. It was… like the tentacle of an octopus… . Last night Col P, the old stinker (read attentively) tried to kiss me but I put my pillow on my face but he pulled it away and started kissing me old beast but when I had got him off I chucked four books as hard as I could at him and hit my mark and then I called for a sponge and a basin of water and a towel to wash my face. He did not get at me to kiss for a long time.

Colonel P had also tried his luck with Esme's friend Joyce, who was travelling with them, but not in such an overt way. The letter clearly worried her parents because a few days later she writes:

I am sorry my letter upset you and Daddy. I was very upset myself then but I think it will be alright now…. I do keep with Miss L as much as I can. I always walk with her when we go out for walks. No, Col P did not kiss me as he had Joyce. That is why I objected to it. I don't mind much any man kissing me ordinarily. I am quite sure it is not through want of trying that he has failed to produce any progeny.

Joyce and Esme at Lady Sandeman's tangi.

And that put Col P firmly in his place. But he wasn't the only pest on the journey: Esme found the insect life less than tolerable.

I kept on waking up during the night with a wretched mosquito buzzing around me. This morning my eyes are covered with bites, my eyebrows, my hands, my elbows, my arms, my legs, all over my face and my body. Yesterday we all went to Lady Sandeman's *tangi* [a dramatic waterfall near Ziarat] there was only one donkey and of course I did not use it very much. J was the first to get on. After she had been on some time, I was allowed to have a ride for about half the distance she had been then the ground was too rough to ride much more after she had ridden again. After a while we got to the *tangi*. There was a lovely little pool of water around the corner as I stayed behind and drank lustily. Then we went up a ladder and got to a little stream and then we got to the funnel where the water came down. It was only coming down in one place but nearly everywhere the walls were as smooth as possible. It was very nice and cool there and Col P took some photographs. I rode first coming back because we tossed and I won but much good it did it do me for when I got off to lead the donkey up a steep hill, Joyce seized it and mounted and rode all the way back from there. I suppose I had ridden 200 yards altogether. My goodness, I was tired when we got home.

Great-Uncle Alick's Fish Pie (Sir Alexander Campbell, 4th Baronet of Barcaldine)

2 fillets fish
8oz new potatoes, washed with their skins left on
sliced thinly
2 medium onions, peeled and finely chopped
1 clove garlic, peeled and finely chopped
½ – ¾ teaspoons fennel seeds (optional)
scant ¼ teaspoon dried chilli flakes
salt and pepper
2 units olive oil
1 glass white wine
1 lemon

Lay the potato slices onto the bottom of a buttered dish followed by the onions and then the tomatoes. Add garlic, fennel seeds and chilli. Season and drizzle over some good olive oil. Bake for 15–20 minutes until the potatoes are almost done. Remove from the oven and add the fish fillets. Pour in the wine and add sliced lemon and little more olive oil. Bake a further 15 minutes. Serve immediately.

Great-Uncle Alick's Fish Ragout

Peel, chop and drain five small tomatoes and put them in a saucepan with one small, chopped onion, a tablespoon of Worcestershire sauce and two tablespoons of olive oil. Season with salt and pepper and cook for 20 minutes. Then add 2 lbs fish cut in pieces, cover closely and simmer for 25 minutes. Very good.

17

JUTLAND

Douglas wrote this during his final years at Dartmouth Royal Naval College and it is particularly tragic in the light of what the future held: 'Please, can I learn swimming? I suppose I must because I am going to be a sailor.'

Alick was disenchanted with the army and did not want his son to follow in his footsteps. Neither did he wish him to enter the church as many of the male Begbies had done previously (one was Archdeacon of Sydney, Australia in the late 1800s, another was Suffragan Bishop, also of Sydney), so the only occupation left 'for a gentleman of his class' was the Royal Navy. On this basis, Alick sent Douglas to Osborne House, the junior officer's training school on the Isle of Wight, then to the Royal Naval College, Dartmouth in Devon. On 21 April 1914, Emily wrote to Duncan:

> Douglas likes Dartmouth very much. He won a tiny cup for a race by a stroke of luck and was photographed when receiving it – an admirable likeness.

Emily's grandson passed out as senior cadet aged fifteen and, commissioned as a mid-shipman, sailed on HMS *Invincible* to the Falklands where he saw action against Admiral von Tirpitz, founder of the German Imperial Navy.

On 13 December 1914 in a letter to Duncan, Emily writes:

Douglas receiving his trophy at Dartmouth Naval College.

One loses touch with one's relatives when one is exiled for years – a fact I realise more now (having returned from India to England) than I had at the time. You will be interested to know that my grandson Douglas, also a cousin of ours Hope Begbie, were in it [referring to a recent victory over the Germans] as the *Invincible* went with Sir F Sturdee's [Vice-Admiral Sir Frederick Charles Doveton Sturdee] squadron a few weeks ago. We did not expect the first news of them to be so satisfactory but it will be long before we get any details. Douglas has been lucky as he was also in the Heligoland fight. I suppose the war will last a long time yet – the loss of valuable lives has been great. Both my sons-in-law [Alick and Cecil] are back with the Army, both expecting any day to be ordered to the Front.

Douglas sailed from South America to fight in Europe. The following is an extract from *The Battle of Jutland, Official Dispatches with Appendixes dated 18 June 1916, from the Commander-in-Chief:*

No. 139fi/H.F. 0022.

"Iron Duke,"

Sir, 18th June 1916.

Be pleased to inform the Lords Commissioners of the Admiralty that in accordance – with the instructions contained in their Lordships' telegram No. 434 of 30th May, Code time' 1740, the Grand Fleet proceeded to sea on 30th May 1916.

2. The instructions given to those portions of the fleet that was not in company with my flag at Scapa Flow were, as follows :

To Vice-Admiral Sir Thomas Jerram, with Second Battle Squadron at Invergordon:

"Leave as soon as ready. Pass through Lat. 58° 15' N., Long. 2° 0' E., meet me 2.0 p.m. to-morrow 31st, Lat. 57° 45' N., Long. 4° 15' E. Several enemy submarines known to be in North Sea."

Acknowledge.

1930 (Code time).

To Vice-Admiral Sir David Beatty, Commanding the Battle-cruiser fleet at Rosyth, with the Fifth Battle Squadron, Rear Admiral Hugh Evan-Thomas in company :

Urgent, Priority.

Admiralty telegram 1740.

Available vessels. Battle-cruiser Fleet, Fifth Battle Squadron and T.B.D.s including Harwich T.B.D.s proceed to approximate position Lat. 56° 40' N., Long. 5° 0' E. Desirable to economise T.B.D.'s fuel. Presume you will be there about 2.0 p.m. tomorrow 31st. I shall be in about Lat. 57° 45' N., Long. 4° 15' E. by 2.0 p.m. unless delayed by fog.

Third Battle Cruiser Squadron, "Chester" and "Canterbury" will leave with me. I will send them on to your rendezvous. If no news by 2.0 p.m. stand towards me to get in visual touch.

I will steer for Horn Reef from position Lat. 57° 45 'N., Long 4° 15' E. Repeat back rendezvous.

The German organisation at night is very good. Their system of recognition signals is excellent. Ours is practically nil. Their searchlights are superior to ours and they use them with great efficiency. Finally, their method of firing at night gives excellent results. I am reluctantly compelled of the opinion that under night conditions we have a great deal to learn from them. Once we commence hitting, the German gunnery falls off but – as shown by the rapidity with which the *Invincible* was sunk at a later stage, their ships are able to fire with great accuracy even when they have received severe punishment.

On 31 May 1916, HMS *Invincible* was sunk at the Battle of Jutland after a German shell exploded in the ammunition hatch. The following is an extract from *The Official History, Naval Operations* by Sir Julian S Corbett, 1923.

Officers and Men Killed in Action HMS *Invincible*, Jutland Bank, 31 May 1916. At 6.32 Admiral Beatty reached his station ahead of the battle fleet. Ahead of him again was Admiral Hood with his three battle cruisers, leading the fleet, and leading it in a manner worth of the honoured name he bore. Upon him was concentrated the fire of three or four of Admiral Hipper's five ships. Under pressure of the oncoming British Dreadnoughts they had turned again to the southward. For the past ten minutes the action between them and the *Invincible* had been growing hot upon similar courses and Admiral Hood with Captain A L Cay, his flag-captain, at his side was directing it from the bridge. Having the advantage of the light he was giving more than he received. The range was down below 9000 yards, but it was the greatest that visibility would permit, and he was doing too well to alter. 'Several shells,' says Commander von Hase of the *Derfflinger,* 'pierced our ship with a terrific force and exploded with a tremendous roar, which shook every seam and rivet. The captain had again frequently to steer the ship out of the line to get clear of the hail of fire.'

So heavy was the punishment he was inflicting, that Admiral Hood hailed Commander Dannreuther, his gunnery officer, in the control top, and called to him, 'Your firing is very good. Keep at it as quickly as you can. Every shot is telling.' They were the last words he is known to have spoken. Just then the mist was riven and from the *Derfflinger* her tormentor was suddenly silhouetted against a light patch of sky. Then as another salvo from the *Invincible* straddled her she began rapid salvoes in reply, in which probably the *Konig* joined with as many. One after another they went home on the *Invincible*. Flames shot up from the gallant flagship, and there came again the awful spectacle of a fiery burst, followed by a huge column of dark smoke, which, mottled with blackened debris, swelled up hundreds of feet in the air, and the mother of all battle cruisers had gone to join the other two that were no more. As her two consorts swerved round her seething death-bed they could see she was rent in two; her stem and stern rose apart high out of the troubled waters as though she had touched the bottom, and nearby a group of half a dozen men were clinging to a life raft, cheering the ships as they raced by to continue the fight. So, in the highest exultation of battle – doing all a man could do for victory – the intrepid Admiral met his end, gilding in his death with new lustre the immortal name of Hood…

Out of the *Invincible*'s crew of over a thousand men, only six survived, Douglas one of the casualties. In the thirteenth-century church of St Bartholomew in Waltham, Kent is a memorial dedicated to parishioners of the village who perished in WWI and, heading the list of seven men engraved in the marble is: Midshipman Douglas A C Birch Royal Navy. He was seventeen years old. Roger told me that, every year on the occasion of the anniversary of the Battle of Jutland, Nell went into mourning.

Midshipman Douglas Alexander Colvin Birch.

Devilled Eggs

4 eggs
½oz butter
¼ pint stock
a little pepper
½ teaspoonful salt
½ teaspoonful cayenne
1 teaspoonful mustard
1 unit Worcestershire sauce
1 teaspoonful finely chopped onions.

Boil the eggs till hard, dip into cold water and remove shells. Cut each through the middle into two halves. Slip out the yolks, and cut a tiny piece off the pointed end of each half white, so that the pieces may stand up like cups. Mash the yolks into a paste with half the butter, a very little salt, a little pepper and the ½ teaspoonful of cayenne. Fill the paste back into the whites of the eggs and arrange them neatly in a dish.

Fry the onions in the remainder of the butter, and as soon as they brown put in the salt, mustard and sauce, which should be mixed together before adding to the onions. Stir all these together over the fire for three to four minutes. Then add the stock thoroughly heated, stir together, pour over the eggs and serve at once.

18

SPIRITUAL DABBLINGS

Nell considered herself to be 'fey' having the gift of second sight and loved nothing better than passing an afternoon experimenting with the paranormal with Esme and my mother, continuing with this pastime when they moved to New Zealand in the 1930s. By all accounts, Nell did experience psychic phenomena and regularly was subjected to bouts of automatic writing, including being 'taken over' by a French nun who signed herself Amélie. The scribblings sometimes covered several pages and were always in French. Nell would also enjoy sessions of table turning. This involved a small circular Kashmiri table made from papier mâché inlaid with mother-of-pearl, which they nicknamed, heaven knows why, Sandy MacPherson.

A question would be asked of Sandy and if the reply was a 'Yes', the table leg would tap once on the floor. If the answer was 'No', it would tap twice. Ma said that on some occasions the table lifted off the ground completely unaided and they had to get up from their chairs to follow it around the room. They also used a *planchette*, which they called Basil. Translated from the French as 'small plank', the board, usually heart-shaped, was used to spell out messages or answer questions. In the case of Nell and her friends, the letters of the alphabet (taken from the Scrabble set) would be placed in a circle, a small piece of paper with 'No' written on it placed halfway, and another with 'Yes' immediately opposite. Once Basil was positioned in the middle of the circle of letters the 'players' would each rest a finger very lightly on the board, which is then supposed to move through unseen forces, nudging the letters to spell out an answer or across to 'Yes' or 'No'.

In a letter to her mother dated 25 March 1912, when she was staying in Shanklin on the Isle of Wight, Esme writes:

On Saturday Miss and Master (Terence, aged fifteen – just) St John came to tea. On Tuesday Eileen came in from a walk, very excited, showing me some visiting cards she had picked up on the shore. They had 'Mrs S Kenning' on them for the most part, and were black-edged. She evidently kept a school as 'Clevedon House School, Ben Rhydding' [near Leeds] was on them. I enclose one. E says they were neatly tied together with string. After tea on Saturday we got onto ghosts somehow and then to table turning and planchette. Miss St John said she did not believe in the two latter. E said planchette had told her many true things, and we proceeded to get dear Basil out and provided him with volumes of paper. For a while we asked him questions and he answered them and was flippant, etc. Then suddenly he wrote this:

'Those cards you picked up on the beach belonged to a woman who drowned herself.'

We asked, 'When?'

'About two months ago.'

'Why?'

'Her little boy died of scarlet fever and she went mad, poor thing. She went to a quiet little place in Cornwall and there she did it.'

'What paper and what date did the account of Mrs K's disappearance come out in?'

'Do not bother me with silly questions, my child,' Basil replied.

'Dear Basil, do go on and don't snub me again.'

'Sweet boy I am.'

'No, you are not Basil, you are a naughty boy.'

'*The Yliad Liam*. Read it in the mirror,' was Basil's parting shot.

Esme had many experiences of the paranormal. In a letter to me in 1987 she relates the following:

> I saw Cecil [my grandfather], very young and with a pale skin, walking along between two tall men in dark robes, looking up at them with great animation. He was young and happy and a new person. I called out, 'Hullo, darling' but he did not pay me any attention. But the episode was so clear that I know it really happened.

Esme.

Aunt Charley's Tea Cake

½lb flour
2 units sugar
2 units butter
1 egg
1 teaspoon of cream of tartar
½ teaspoon bicarbonate of soda
milk

Rub butter into flour into which the cream of tartar and bicarbonate of soda have been previously well mixed. Beat up the egg, add milk and make it very moist. Bake in cake tins very well-greased. Bake in a quick oven 15–20 minutes. Glaze with egg when baked. Scones as above but minus the egg and dough thick. Do not roll but pat out with hand to required shape.
Much loved by children of all ages.

19

ROGER AND MA, CHILDREN OF THE RAJ

Ma was born on 12 September 1922 in Nainital in the foothills of the Himalayas. Founded by the British in 1841, at approximately 6000 feet above sea level with forest-covered hills set around Lake Naini (according to the legend, one of the emerald green eyes of Shiva's wife Sati), the gentle climate and scenery made it a popular resort.

Her brother Roger was born eight years later in 1930 in southern India at the Wellington Cantonment Hospital in the Nilgiri Hills.

With their parents frequently away they were looked after by their *ayah* (Indian nanny) and the first words they spoke were in Hindustani. Ma and Roger became very fond of their *ayah*, but when Roger reached the age of five his parents broke with tradition and employed a Miss Adams from England.

Statuesque and solid as an oak, Nanny Adams appeared a fearsome individual to a small person like Roger, but he was no pushover and gave as good as he got, which ending up in him being reprimanded for his behaviour and forced to take long walks, which he hated. There were moments of retribution, however, such as when, during one such punishment, Nanny Adams poked at a baby cobra sunning itself on a jungle path and, to her horror, the snake coiled up her umbrella. Riddled with loneliness, she never adjusted to her situation but was

Above left: *Aunt Charley.*

Top right: *Esme and Ma at two weeks, September 1922.*

Above right: *Ma's first steps.*

Right: *Roger and Ma with their* ayah.

Far right: *Roger having a mud bath.*

fully aware that, if she quit voluntarily, she would have to bear the cost of her passage back to England. Therefore, the only answer in order to get the sack and avoid dipping into her own funds was to be horrid to Roger. This tactic resulted one time in Nanny Adams shoving the little boy onto the concrete floor of the bathroom with such force that a deep scar on Roger's knee remained a permanent reminder of this ill treatment throughout his adult life.

Because of army commitments the family travelled widely across the country, from Rawalpindi, Peshawar and the Shalimar Gardens in Pakistan, to Ahmednagar in the state of Maharashtra in the centre and, for a longer period, to Ootacamund in the deep south, where Ma went to school. It was normal for parents and children to lead virtually separate lives and the only meal they shared was breakfast, which was taken on the verandah. Lunch, or 'tiffin' (a light meal generally taken at midday), and tea would be administered by their *ayah* whilst their parents dined at the Club. In *The Highlands of India* (vol II) by Major-General D J F Newall RA (1887), he says:

> (...) the Shalimar Gardens have so often been described by travellers that they scarcely need notice here, except to say that many a pleasant 'tiffin' did we enjoy in those umbrageous shades, sketch book in hand.

On the rare occasions that my grandparents entertained at home, Ma described how the servants would dress a table for a dinner party: rather than arranging a traditional vase of flowers as a centrepiece, the white damask cloth would be decorated with swirling, intricate patterns made from coloured rice grains and scented petals. Light was provided by candles; to reduce the heat from the flame, decorative paper shades would be supported on small metal holders.

Survival in hostile climes was a day-to-day concern; diseases such as cholera and malaria were prevalent, so no raw food was eaten unless first soaked and disinfected in *'pinki pani'* (*'pinki'* being potassium permanganate, which takes on a rosy hue when diluted, and *'pani'*, the Hindustani for water). In spite of these precautions, little protected

Above left: *My grandfather Cecil with Roger and Nanny Adams in Thandiani.*

Above right: *Ma at the Shalimar Gardens, Kashmir.*

Three generations: Nell, Esme and Bridget, my mama.

them from the bite of the mosquito and, like her father, Ma frequently suffered from malaria, the fever producing delirium and terrifying hallucinations. Once she was convinced that a giant cobra was lying in wait at the foot of her bed ready to pounce, its beady eyes gleaming in the dark. Fear prevented her crying for help and it was only when daylight broke that she saw the 'eyes' were the sparkling diamante buttons on her mother's dancing shoes.

In a letter dated 22 June 1896 to Harriette (Ethel Campbell's sister-in-law, married to John Peter William's son Alexander, 2nd Baronet), Emily writes:

> It's been a very unhealthy spring here and small pox and enteric fever are being prevalent. I expect that cholera has broken out. We are up in the hills now in the Himalaya range where it is beautifully cool and so lovely. We can see the range of mountains. When May [1890–1984 – her and Francis's daughter] first got ill we sent Eric [their son, who became the 6th Baronet] to Emily Begbie, who was at Dehra [Dehradhun]. She, Frank [Ethel's husband Lieutenant-Colonel Francis James Brooke Campbell, 1861–1918] and the whole family are up here. They have taken a house for the season and Frank got six months' leave. They are all very flourishing.

Because of the higher risk of death from disease the children of the Army and Civil Service families were sent England to be schooled, which caused massive upheaval. In another letter to Harriette Campbell, Richard Campbell's wife Nellie writes:

> I have been lousy since I came out. I had a pleasant voyage on the whole though it was certainly very hot. Dick [Richard, her husband] met me at Bombay and was very glad to have me out again, but it is strange to us both to be without the children and they are a great miss in our daily life. However, I am truly glad for their sakes that we did not bring them out, as they are far better [off] in England. We get very good news of them in every mail.

Ma and Nell – great hats!

They must have had a change of heart because, in a letter dated 2 October, 1899 Nellie confirms:

> All our plans are now changed as regards the children. After much thought on the subject we have now decided to take them out to India again for a year or two and I have a house for them in the hills with a nursery governess. We think it is far better for them not to be entirely separated from us while they are still so small. The hill climate is much the same as England except that one does not get the bitter winters.

Lushington Hall in Ootacamund was built circa 1880 first as a summer retreat for a wealthy British businessman and then became Hebron School for Girls in 1899, where Ma was educated for a period. The property was set in more than twenty acres of idyllic gardens and woodland, with lawns and an orchard.

Ootacamund, known by the British as 'Snooty Ooty', is situated at 7349 feet above sea level in the Nilgiri Hills and was founded in the 1800s. It was the most elegant and sophisticated of the southern Indian resorts, with its charming bungalows, quaint cottages and church; and became the summer capital of the Madras Presidency. The climate remains pretty constant throughout the year and Ootacamund was considered extremely healthy for children. However, in 1933, aged eleven and deemed old enough to travel alone by sea, a journey which lasted two weeks, Ma travelled to England to continue her schooling.

St Hilda's in Bexhill-on-Sea was an establishment with only nine pupils. It was run by two women, one of whom sported a spectacular moustache. dressed in loud tweeds and flat brogues. The girls slept outside on a balcony all year round and were fed sweet and savoury sandwiches stacked one above the other in the same tin for lunch every day. Despite this unusual diet, Ma didn't seem to suffer any dire consequences in adult life.

But Ma loved her childhood in India and described in detail the appearance of thousands of jewel-like spiders in the garden after a monsoon deluge, her pet mongoose and other delights. As small

Above left: Ma and little friend being taken to a picnic in Thandiani on a palanquin.

Above right: *Ma in her school uniform, Ootacamund.*

Children who stayed in India – Ahmednagar children's Christmas party c. 1928, Ma second from right.

children we could imagine there being no place on earth more magical. She also told us about the thrill of tiger hunts on elephant back. The following is an extract from *The Asiatic Journal* of January 1828, entitled 'Tiger Excursion at Doongul, near Hyderabad':

After various attempts the first tiger was killed by one of the parties. The tiger having killed a bullock, he was scared away by the people and the carcase left on the spot to allure the tiger. He was later shot by one of the party who was secured in a tree. The second tiger was killed when returned from a morning's hunt, when he suddenly started upon one of the *shikaries* [native guides] whom he threw down by the mere agitation of the air caused by his blow, and the *shikari* received a scratch from his claw. Mr A B [Alfred Begbie, my 4 x great-grandfather], on an elephant, immediately fired both the charges of a double-barrelled gun at the tiger and laid him sprawling on the ground. The fourth tiger offered the most sport which was a small range of low rocks among which he secured himself and repeated his attacks, bounding from rock to rock. Three tigers made their appearance, one of which was fired at and wounded. This tiger disappeared with another and the remaining tiger lodged himself on the rocks. The tiger then made an attack on Mr A B's elephant and Mr A B gave him a shot from his rifle and killed him.

A young handsome woman, who had dressed and ornamented herself for some particular occasion, happening to go a little beyond the precincts of the village was seized by a tiger, but being rather stout and too heavy to be clearly carried off, her limbs were torn off from the waist and the upper part of her body was carried by the tiger about a mile from the place through a thick part of the jungle.

For a brief period during 1935, the family was stationed in Campbellpur, a military base founded in 1904 near Attock in the Punjab district about fifty miles from Peshawar. In late 1935 or early 1936, Ma was summoned from school in Bexhill back to Campbellpur, to where she sailed on the P&O liner SS *Strathnaver*. Roger had previously sailed on the same ship en route for England with their mother Esme, who had to go to

London for an operation, and the sight of Arab dhows drawn up on the sand as they travelled the Suez Canal was etched on his memory. In those days, washing facilities were shared and a steward would draw a bath on a pre-arranged schedule for each passenger. Roger, poor chap and aged only four years old, one day trotted along to the wrong bath on the wrong deck and was extremely upset to find that his mother wasn't there to help him.

My parents on their wedding day, 2 June 1948.

After the war Ma, who had trained as a nurse, wanted to leave New Zealand but tickets were in extremely short supply. One afternoon she, Esme and Nell dusted down Basil the ouija board and asked if there was any likelihood one might come her way. The reply was positive: Basil confirmed without a doubt that she would be granted a passage, even naming the ship, the SS *Rangitiki*. Thinking no more of it, some months later she received a telephone call confirming a berth had been reserved for her on the SS *Rangitata*, the sister ship of SS *Rangitiki*.

Ma continued her career at the old Westminster Hospital in Horseferry Road, London, staying at the weekends with her godfather's family in Sussex. Living next door was a handsome bachelor, Trevor Jarvis, who had recently settled back into civilian life after serving in the RNVR during WWII. They fell in love and were married at the church of St Mary Magdalene, Bolney on 2 June 1948. Dad told us that he was directly descended from the notorious highwayman Dick Turpin. But that's another story...

Andrew Fuse Cocktail

Glass: champaigne [sic] glass smeared with lemon and
dusted with sugar
Base: equal parts: Benedictine, rye whisky, brandy, square gin

This should be mixed in iced shaker.
Topping: suggest chilled dry ginger ale with coiled lemon
and orange peel.

Note: This drink sounds vicious (and is) but it tastes very
~~harmful~~ [sic] harmless. I once gave a teetotal maiden aunt
four in quick succession telling her they were soft drinks.
She cut me out of her will.

APPENDICES

The following explanatory notes are taken from Emily's notebook containing some of her recipes.

INDIAN WEIGHTS AND MEASURES

The unit here is a tablespoon, but any measure either of capacity or weight may be substituted – each egg is counted as two units: white = 1 unit, yolk = 1 unit. Indian eggs are smaller. The unit here in the receipts [recipes] is 1 tablespoon pressed down lightly for solids and as full as it can be for liquids. That is to say, approximately one ounce, if that measure be prepared. This gives a result suitable for two or three people.

For all things that can be measured in a tablespoon, the unit is a tablespoon. 1 *chittack* = 4 tablespoons. For such things, as cannot be measured in a tablespoon the unit is 1oz – this is mostly stock, and 5 units raw meat and 20 units water means 5oz raw meat and 20 tablespoons water.

BASIC COOKING TIPS

Boiling: Meat should be put into water that is boiling furiously, and kept boiling like this for 5 minutes. This makes outside of meat hard and preserves juice inside. After 5 minutes, simmer gently.

Fish: Never use very hot water or the skin will break. Vinegar and salt should always be in the water. To make very good boiling liquor for it: water, vinegar, claret, onions and carrots and a faggot of herbs boiled together and allowed to get cold. Then strain off and use to boil your fish in.

Vegetables: They should be not washed till they are to be cooked and they should be plunged into boiling water into which 1 dessertspoon of salt has been added to 1 quart of water. The saucepan should be uncovered and they should boil furiously.

Peas & beans: They require a teaspoonful of sugar in addition to the salt.

Potatoes: They should always be put in cold water and only just enough to cover them and after first boil cannot simmer too slowly. They require at least one hour to dry after the water has been drained off.

Soufflés: To prevent sinking. Place on dish on which there is heated salt. Wonderful in its effects.

Soups: To remove fat: dip a clean dinner napkin in cold water, wring it out and drop on surface of broth. Remove.

Coffee: Warm jug. Put in coffee. Pour boiling water and <u>beat</u> with wooden spoon till the grounds sink.

Cake or loaf when stale: To make fresh: throw a teacup of water into a hot oven. Place the cake or loaf in the oven, shut the door and in ten minutes it will be quite fresh. There is no fear of rusting oven.

Cake, to prevent sticking to a tin: Place the tin on a damp cloth when you take it out of the oven and the cake will be in no danger of sticking.

Cake, to keep moist: Place in a tin with a thick slice of bread at the top and bottom of the tin. The bread will become hard as a rock. The cake having drained all the moisture away from the bread will be quite fresh. Or place butterproof paper all round the tin and put the cake in it.

To prevent illness, all uncooked food (salads, fruit, etc.) was given a brief soak in *pinki pani,* the name given to a dilute solution of potassium permanganate, which was lethal to micro-organisms.

Receipt for a Fashionable Route.

TABLE OF PROPORTIONS

BATTER	Baked or boiled: 4 units flour, 4 units eggs, 16 units milk.
FRYING BATTER	1 unit flour, 2 liquid, 1 egg, ¼oz oil.
SOUFFLE BATTER	1 unit flour, 1 unit water, ¼ unit butter, 1 egg. This has to be boiled before frying.
CAKES	A standard cake: 16 units self-raising flour, 12 units sugar, 8 units butter, 5 eggs
CUSTARDS	Baked: 3 eggs to 20 units milk. Bake 8–20 minutes.
GELATINE	Jellies and creams: 2 units chip or 1 unit ground gelatine to 20 units liquid; cream 2 or 1 to 24
FARINES	Cornflour: 1½ units to 20 of liquid. Rice: 8 to 20. Sago: 4 to 20. Ground rice: 6 to 20. Tapioca: 3 to 20.
MEAT MOULDS	Raw meat: 1 unit to 2 milk or stock. Cooked meat: 2 units meat, 1 unit panade, 1 unit milk, ½ unit egg.
MILK PUDDINGS:	Cornflour: 1 unit to 20 units liquid. Arrowroot: 1 to 20. Rice: 3 to 20. Sago, semolina and tapioca: 2 to 20. Macaroni and vermicelli: 4 solid to 20.
PASTRY	Puff: 4 units butter to 4 units flour. Medium: 3 units butter to 4 units flour. Family: 2 units butter to 4 units flour. Short: 2 units butter, 4 units flour, 1 unit sugar. Suet: 5 units suet to 8 units flour.
STOCK	Ordinary: 16 units meat or fish (solid) to 44 units liquid. Add 8 units meat for best consommés.
THICKENING	Soups: ½ to one unit flour to 44 units liquid. Ordinary sauces: 1 unit flour, 1 unit butter to 15 units liquid. Thick: 1 unit flour, 1 unit butter to 12 units liquid. Thin: I unit flour, I unit butter to 20 units liquid.

INDEX

Find out more about RedDoor
Press and sign up to our
newsletter to hear about our
latest releases, author events,
exciting **competitions**
and more at

reddoorpress.co.uk

YOU CAN ALSO FOLLOW US:

 @RedDoorBooks

 Facebook.com/RedDoorPress

 @RedDoorBooks